LIGHTHEARTED

MINIDRAMAS

FOR CHURCHES

A MESSAGE IN · A MINUTE

WILLIAM D. WOLFE
WITH
SHERYL J. ANDERSON

Judson Press ® Valley Forge

Library of Congress Cataloging-in-Publication Data
Wolfe, William D., 1954–
   A message in a minute : lighthearted minidramas for churches / by
William D. Wolfe and Sheryl J. Anderson Parrott.
   p.   cm.
   ISBN 0-8170-1181-1
   1. Christian drama, American.   2. Drama in public worship.
I. Anderson Parrott, Sheryl J., 1958–   . II. Title.
PS3573.O5268M4   1992
812'.54 — dc20
                                                                           92-5618
                                                                           CIP

Acknowledgments

I cannot claim this book as being MINE. I must acknowledge the help, patience, and support of a number of people.

First of all, there is the support and encouragement that I have received from my family. My wife, Carol, and our three children, Kecia, David, and Lizi have allowed me to put in the many extra hours of writing and rewriting to make this manuscript complete. They have been very patient with "Dad" as I pecked away page after page, night after night.

Next comes my church family, the First Baptist Church of Mason, Michigan. Their openness has allowed me to write minidramas and incorporate them into our worship services. The saying goes that the seven last words of the church are "we've never done it that way before." My church family, on the other hand, has gone in the other direction with its seven tough words for ministry: "Who says we can't do that here!"

I also want to thank Sheryl Anderson for her work as the "rewriter." She took many of these minidramas and added fire to them, like turning a subcompact car into a racing machine. She saw the good things; but, as my youngest child says, "She made them gooder"!

Finally, I send many thank-yous to the members of the drama troupe of Mason First Baptist for their time, talents, and energies in bringing these minidramas from the silence of the page to the life of the stage. You people are great! We've even had fun doing it.

Contents

From the Epistles

Introduction

Professional training and experience in dramatics are not prerequisites for use of the minidramas in this book. They are written for use by anyone who would like to "put some drama" in their church. Almost all of these skits have already been performed by the nonprofessional drama troupe of the church I pastor. They were received well and added to the worship experience or group gathering.

These minidramas are designed to require minimal stage props; at most, a table and chairs will be needed. At times the stage directions may mention more elaborate props, but tables, chairs, or other simple props can be substituted for convenience. The number of people needed ranges from one to eleven. Most require a cast of just two or three.

Here are a few tips for effectively using these minidramas in your church.

1. Planning and preparation. Make assignments about a month ahead. The amount of preparation time that is needed will vary according to the experience of your cast members. An experienced cast may only need a few days of preparation, while novices may require several weeks.

2. Adapting characters. Almost all of these skits can be adapted to fit the cast members that are available. For instance, with few or no changes, many parts can be played by either a man or a woman. As a general rule, children under ten should not be given speaking parts; if a script calls for a small child, ask an older child or young person to pretend to be younger.

3. Learning lines. If you plan to have cast members memorize their lines, remember that some people have an easy time learning their lines while others struggle. A prompter can be placed in the front row or close to the action. Many of these skits allow a person to have a book, newspaper, or table in front of him or her. Scripts can be concealed there and will be fairly unnoticeable to those watching. This is also helpful if it is not possible for the cast members to memorize their lines. Even if lines are not memorized, the performers should be familiar with their lines and comfortable in delivering them.

4. Coordination with the pastor. Find out from the pastor what upcoming sermon themes will be, and coordinate the use of minidramas with these themes. The pastor also should have the final say as to where a minidrama is to be placed in the worship service.

5. Placement in the worship service. Minidramas can be a hindrance to worship if they are placed in an inappropriate spot. When deciding where to place a minidrama in a worship service, it's important to strive for smooth transitions. In some situations the minidrama might be placed at the beginning of the service, even before the first hymn is sung. Others might fit best right before the sermon. If props will need to be set up and taken down, this should be a consideration in the placement of the minidrama.

6. Choosing performance space. These minidramas can be performed in the main aisle, in the front or on the platform, or even while moving around the sanctuary. In deciding on the best place, it is important to consider sight lines, traffic patterns (of cast members, the congregation, and other worship service participants), and acoustics. Depending on the layout of your place of worship, the need for certain props may determine where the skit is performed.

7. Using minidramas in other settings. Some of these minidramas can easily be incorporated into other church functions. Church business meetings can be livened up a bit.

Congregational dinners can have a little extra sparkle with two or three skits added. Youth meetings, retreats, and even Sunday church school classes can benefit from an occasional minidrama or two. Be creative and be bold.

8. Writing for your situation. You may want to use drama to address themes and issues that are not covered in this book. Someone in your church may want to write minidramas. You may want to try writing one yourself. Beginning writers will need a few guidelines: It is best to begin with only a few characters; each minidrama should try to make one point, not many; each minidrama should have a beginning, a middle, and an end; simple, spoken language is most effective (it can help to read aloud as you write); and simple props and stage directions work best. Don't let a lack of experience keep you from trying, and don't be frustrated if your first efforts aren't Academy Award caliber. With some practice and persistence, you may very well be surprised by the end results.

Remember that minidramas can help bring the truths of the Bible alive. If you can do this, you will have accomplished great things.

Noah's Daughters

Character: Noah
Costume: Robe of the period

(NOAH enters with a clipboard. He checks off several items and heaves a deep sigh.)

NOAH: Okay. That's two one-hump camels, two toucans, and two three-toed sloths. The promenade level is filled, and there's not a whole lot of room left on the fiesta deck. This is going to be one full ark.

Lord, can we talk? You'll recall that you didn't give me a whole lot of choice about accepting this assignment. You'll recall that I decided to accept anyway, you being the Lord God Almighty and all. So, I figure I get points for being a good sport right off the bat. But let's not push it, okay? I understand that this is not a pleasure cruise. I understand that someone has to feed the birds and slop the hogs and clean up after the elephants, and it might as well be me. I'll accept that. Let it rain until the next millennium, and I will keep a neat and orderly ark and bear my trials with grace. Except for one thing: What am I going to do with my daughters?

A mighty task is one thing, but spending more than two hours cooped up in a little boat with two teenage girls is more than even you should ask of me! Why do you test me this way, Lord? People are laughing at me. Not because I have a ship filled with animals in my front yard, miles from the nearest dock. They're laughing because they know these two girls are going to drive me crazy!

Really, Lord, have you considered all the alternatives? Maybe a separate little boat for them? They wouldn't have to row. I'd tow them along behind, but at least they'd have their space. And I'd have my sanity!

I'm willing to accept whatever rare and exotic animals you send me, Lord, but these two are creatures of a completely different stripe—strange birds. They don't even speak the same language I do. I told them about this trip, and they said, "We're fresh, my man. It's a def trip and it sounds bad." What does that mean? The chimpanzees make more sense!

And have you seen this list? This is what they want to bring with them: suntan lotion, curling irons, makeup in every color of the rainbow, rollerblades, blue jeans, and a volleyball net.

If I expect them to work, they want seven dollars an hour. And they won't do anything that might make them chip their nail polish—as though you can groom a water buffalo without getting a little dirt under your fingernails!

Can't we work out a deal? Maybe you could find a little dry patch where they could stay, and I'll come back and pick them up—in about fifteen years. In the meantime I can tend to these fine specimens you've entrusted to my care without a bunch of rotten comments from the peanut gallery. I run a tight ship. I want people who are going to work with me, not against me. I want people with sense, with dedication to their task, with compassion and understanding.

(There is a crack of thunder. NOAH holds his hand out and reacts to the raindrops that are beginning to fall.)

Rain. Lots of rain. I see.

On the other hand, this might be a good experiment in communal living. Force us to get to know one another, learn to respect each other's differences, learn to value our differences. You're right as always, Lord. This will be good for us. We'll have a good time. You understand that I wasn't complaining, right? I was just examining my options. My extremely limited options. No problem here, Lord. We're ready to sail away. Let it rain, let it rain, let it rain!

(He hurries away.)

I'm Not Going Down There

Characters: Abe, Razpah
Costumes: Robes of the period

(ABE and RAZPAH enter, both carrying large bags on their shoulders. They walk to center and look out in awe. RAZPAH's expression slowly changes to one of delight, but ABE's changes to one of fear. RAZPAH takes Abe's arm and starts to lead him down an aisle. ABE hangs back, pulling his arm out of Razpah's grasp with a sharp movement.)

ABE: Let's think about this a minute.

RAZPAH: What's to think about? We're going to get left behind. Let's go!

ABE: I don't know about this, Razpah.

RAZPAH: Oh, come on, Abe! Moses said that the Lord Almighty is holding these waters back.

ABE: I know what Moses said. I also know that this is the same guy who said God changed his staff into a snake. I mean, really. How much do we know about this guy?

RAZPAH: O ye of little faith, Abe!

ABE: O me of little lung capacity. The Red Sea is pretty wide, Razpah. Do you think I'm going to be able to hold my breath if those walls of water come crashing down when we're halfway across?

RAZPAH: Moses said, "Do not be afraid. Stand firm and you will see the deliverance the LORD will bring you today."[1]

ABE: Let's define the term "deliverance." Where exactly are we being delivered to? Are you sure we're not being delivered to a mass baptism? What if we get out there and the Lord says, "Surprise"?

(ABE makes a gesture illustrating two halves of the sea coming together violently and brings his hands together with a loud, final clap. RAZPAH shakes his head and sighs patiently.)

RAZPAH: Honestly, Abe. You whine more than Pharaoh did when he got "frogged." We're going to be fine. Just put a little trust in God.

ABE: God I trust. No problem there. It's the water that I'm having a little trouble trusting. After all, this is a liquid we're discussing. H_2O. Stuff that's supposed to flow—the way it flows out of our fishing nets. The fish stay put, and the water flows. And speaking of staying put . . .

RAZPAH: Abe, we have to cross. Listen. Keep your eyes forward. Just don't look at the water.

ABE: Don't look at the water? With it stacked up above my head at least a mile high? Don't look at the water? I suppose that's what you say to your cracker just before you dunk it in a steaming bowl of soup—"Just don't look at the soup." Look or not, that cracker's sunk.

RAZPAH: Then I suppose you're going to stay here and deal with Pharaoh—by yourself.

ABE: No, I thought I'd hang around and see if God might build a bridge.

RAZPAH: This is a bridge. It just goes along the bottom of the sea, not across it.

ABE: What kind of a bridge is that? Okay, okay. I don't expect God to build me a bridge. A little boat will be just fine. Nothing too fancy. Your basic sailboat. Actually, a rowboat would do in a pinch. All right, I'll take a small raft—just as long as it floats!

RAZPAH: Let me get this straight. You aren't willing to show that you have faith in God, but you still expect God to make a boat just for you? Get with the program, Abe. This is your chance to cross. Period. Grin and bear it.

---

[1]Exodus 14:13

(ABE does his best to grin, but the smile quickly fades into a miserable grimace.)

ABE: Isn't there some other way I can prove my faith? What if I do one hundred push-ups every day for the rest of my life? No, no, I'll diet every sabbath. No, no, I'll let my hair grow down to my waist. Those would be great statements of faith. Wouldn't they please the Lord?

RAZPAH: Abe, I'm not into great statements of faith. I'm into doing as the Lord asks. I don't make the tests, I take them and trust that I'll pass. Now, come on before we get passed by.

ABE: Just a minute.

(ABE takes a pair of water wings out of his bag and pulls them on. RAZPAH watches in amazement. His amazement grows as ABE pulls a rain poncho out of the bag and slips it on.)

RAZPAH: This doesn't look much like the armor of faith.

ABE: I'm just taking a few precautions. I mean, walking across the bottom of the sea is new for all of us. I'm preparing for the unexpected.

RAZPAH: Pharaoh is the one who needs to prepare for the unexpected. He thought the frogs were bizarre. Wait until he sees the nation of Israel walking across the bottom of the sea. And unless we hurry, we're going to be here to point them out. Let's go.

ABE: You want some water wings? I have an extra pair.

RAZPAH: I have all the protection I need. Didn't you hear a word Moses said?

(RAZPAH marches down the aisle. ABE hurries after him, rummaging in his bag.)

ABE: Wait a minute. You mean to tell me that you bought all that milk and honey stuff? Razpah, all this talk about liquids makes me nervous. Let's talk about solids for a change—dry things. Hey, do you have my flippers?

(ABE races down the aisle after RAZPAH.)

Exterior View

Characters: Sara, Tim, Ethel
Costumes: Contemporary

(TIM, SARA, and ETHEL enter and stop center stage. They are all looking offstage at the same thing. They try to be subtle about their staring, but they are not.)

SARA: There's no way you're going to convince me to vote for that man as our new pastor.

TIM: Sara! What's wrong with him?

SARA: Really, Tim. Just look at him.

ETHEL: Get a load of that hair. Look at his face. And he's short, too! He's just about the most unimpressive minister I've ever laid my eyes on.

TIM: That's just the outside, Ethel. I'm sure that given the chance he'd be a wonderful pastor for us.

SARA: Tim, how is a man who can't control his hair going to control a congregation? Hmmm? He can't get his hair to poof up in front like a good TV evangelist. What does that say about him? We can't expect new people to be interested in our church if our pastor can't even poof his hair.

ETHEL: And we need someone who stands six foot two, minimum, so that when he stands in the pulpit, people sit up and take notice. That guy would get lost behind the pulpit Bible. I can't believe they even let a pipsqueak like that into seminary.

TIM: You mean God doesn't call short people.

SARA: Ethel has a point, Tim. People aren't going to come to church to see a puny, under-sized nerd deliver the word of the almighty God. And it's not as though he's just short. He's plain, too.

TIM: Is this a call committee or a beauty pageant?

SARA: There's no need to get snippy, Tim. It's just that if you're going to look at a guy every Sunday, he should at least be pleasant to look at. How can you concentrate on the man's sermon if all you can think about is that he really needs to do something with his hair?

ETHEL: We need someone good looking and charming. Like Reverend Leroy on TV.

TIM: Let me get this straight. You two are going to vote against this candidate because he doesn't have poofed hair, is a little on the short side, and doesn't look like Tom Selleck.

ETHEL: Where have you been, Tim? Tom Selleck is old hat. We need Tom Cruise in a collar. Johnny Depp in vestments.

TIM: I don't care if you want Jerry Lewis in a tutu! Don't you see how ridiculous you're being? You're turning your back on the person that God has sent to lead our church just because he isn't pinup material? That strikes me as downright narrow-minded, not to mention un-Christian.

SARA: Does it? How interesting. How did it strike you when we offered to fix you up with Gloria Smith and you said you wouldn't date her because she's chubby?

TIM: That . . . was . . . different.

ETHEL: What do you mean by "different"?

TIM: It wasn't a physical thing at all. We were just . . . incompatible. That's right, incompatible. I mean, what's the point in trying to start a relationship when you know you're going to be incompatible?

(SARA and ETHEL watch him silently. TIM smiles nervously. TIM takes a good, long look offstage at the pastor then turns back to the women.)

TIM *(CONT)*: You know, now that you mention it, he is a little short. And we do need a pastor we can look up to.

(The trio exits.)

TIM *(CONT)*: Maybe if he could just get his hair to poof. That would be a start. And make his whole look . . . different. All excellent points, ladies. We need the right person with the right look. Excellent points.

God's Will for Your Life

Characters: Howard, Brad, Irene
Costumes: Contemporary

(Brad and Irene are sitting at a cafeteria table, eating and chatting. Howard rushes up, full of excitement.)

Howard: You are never going to guess what happened. *(Brad and Irene look at him with interest.)* Guess.

Irene: You said we wouldn't be able to, Howard.

Howard: Okay, then I'll tell you. Is this weird or what? I was standing outside Mason State Bank, and I looked up and the new clock there said 1:13.

Irene: You're right, Howard. We never would have guessed.

Howard: Wait! There's more. I ran over to Schmidt's to get a quart of lemonade—because I'm trying to cut down on my caffeine intake, you know—and guess how much that quart of lemonade cost me.

Irene: Your turn, Brad.

Brad: A dollar fifty?

Howard: No! One dollar and thirteen cents! And then I remembered that when I was at the Spartan Speedway Friday night—well, guess the number of the car that won the featured race.

Irene: I'm going out on a limb here, but—113?

Howard: Yes! Can you believe it?

Brad: What's to believe? You went to lunch late, lemonade is on sale, and you're a race fan.

Howard: Don't you see? God is telling me something.

Irene: My turn again. God is telling you that the world is going to end at 1:13 PM on January thirteenth and that we'd best straighten up our acts by then or God will stomp us into individual pancakes. Or something along those lines. Am I close?

Howard: Not at all. You think I'm running around seeing signs of Armageddon? Don't be silly. God is simply telling me that the winning lottery number today will be 113. *(Irene and Brad look at him in silent wonder.)* Don't you see it?

Brad: Howard, you can't be serious.

Howard: Oh, I am. Completely. This is God's way of telling me that I should put some money on the lottery today. And obviously, since God has gone to all this trouble to point this out to me, I'm going to win. It's as clear as water in a stream.

Irene: I think you have a little algae running in your stream, Howard.

Howard: What's that supposed to mean?

Brad: Howard, think for a minute. Aren't you being a little silly?

Howard: You don't believe that God uses signs to show us the way?

Brad: Sure, I believe that. But I also believe that some people like to find signs to help them believe what they want—and then they put the responsibility for their actions on God.

Howard: So you're saying it's my fault God put lemonade on sale this week.

Irene: Ask Mr. Schmidt what he thinks of that theory.

Brad: Howard, do you really think that God cares whether or not you win the lottery? If God's showing you a sign, don't you think it would be about something a little more important?

Howard: I think the lottery's pretty big stuff—especially if I win.

IRENE: But it's not big stuff to God. Maybe God wants you to look at hymn 113. Or read Psalm 113.

HOWARD: Now why would God do that?

IRENE: Maybe there's a message there for you. One besides how to win the lottery.

BRAD: We're not denying that God might have a message for you, Howard. We're just saying that you have to be awfully careful when you designate something as being God's will. And you still have to be willing to take responsibility for your actions—no matter whose will you're following.

HOWARD: Well, you've made your feelings clear. We'll discuss this again—after I win the lottery—and we'll see who has the last laugh. Maybe it's God's will that I win, so that you'll learn something.

(HOWARD marches off indignantly. BRAD and IRENE watch him go, then turn back to each other.)

IRENE: And maybe it's God's will that some people never quite get the message.

Saying Grace

Characters: Pop, Mom, Fred, Shirlean
Costumes: Contemporary

(POP, MOM, and FRED are at the dinner table, ready to eat.)

MOM: *(calling)* Shirlean!

SHIRLEAN: *(offstage)* I'm coming!

POP: You've been saying that for five minutes. Get in here now or you don't eat.

SHIRLEAN: *(offstage)* What are we eating anyway?

POP: Get in here now!

SHIRLEAN: *(offstage)* Oh, great. Must be something really delicious.

MOM: Shirlean, do you want to be grounded for the rest of the month?

SHIRLEAN: *(entering)* I'm here, I'm here.

(SHIRLEAN takes her place at the table. FRED smiles at her with smug superiority; she glares back.)

FRED: Pop, can we go for ice cream after dinner tonight? Maybe get sundaes at Dairy King?

POP: Ice cream isn't free, you know. Besides we just went for ice cream the other night.

FRED: It wasn't the other night, Pop. It was Fourth of July.

SHIRLEAN: And we got a lecture about the high cost of living then too.

MOM: Shirlean, don't be disrespectful.

POP: They don't know how else to be. I break my back to keep a roof over their heads, and all I ever hear from these kids is "Give me this" and "I want that" and "Why can't I?" Some gratitude. I give up everything and get nothing in return. Thanks a whole lot, kids.

SHIRLEAN: Wait a minute. We do things. We clean up our rooms. We take out the trash.

MOM: After I ask you six or seven times.

POP: And when was the last time you did anything without being asked?

FRED: I do my homework without being told.

POP: You must not do it very well if your last report card is any judge.

FRED: Algebra is really hard. If you'd help me, maybe I'd do a little better.

POP: Oh, so now I have to give you an allowance, put food on the table, and do your homework! That's some pretty cushy deal you've got going, young man.

MOM: Enough arguing. I didn't work all evening on this meal to let it get cold. Someone say grace.

(They all fold their hands and look at each other. POP sighs and bows his head. The others follow suit.)

POP: Dear Lord, we thank you for this food that you have provided for us in your love. We don't deserve this bounty, and we are grateful that you love us enough to give it to us anyway. Amen.

(All raise their heads and grab for the food except FRED. He keeps his hands folded and stares at the table.)

MOM: Fred, quit playing around. Pass the potatoes.

FRED: We say grace every night, and I've never thought about it until now. Grace. Giving thanks for the love we receive whether we deserve it or not. Loving whether others deserve it or not. We say the word every night, and I've never really heard it before.

(MOM, POP and SHIRLEAN quietly fold their hands again and look at each other sadly. FRED bows his head. The others follow suit.)

FRED: Lord, give us grace. Teach us grace. Help us learn it. Help us live it.

ALL: Amen.

Running From the IRS

Characters: Jonah, Agent Hooper, Flight Announcer (offstage)
Costumes: Contemporary

(JONAH stands in line at an airport check-in counter. He wears an overcoat and carries a suitcase in one hand and his ticket in the other. He is nervous and impatient, checking his watch frequently. As the FLIGHT ANNOUNCER begins to speak, JONAH listens with growing agitation.)

FLIGHT ANNOUNCER: *(offstage)* Your attention, please. Flight 1670 is now available for boarding. All passengers with small children, special needs, or those in a bigger hurry than the rest of us, may now board the aircraft through gate eleven. Calling Flight 1670 to Tarshish with continuing service to Barcelona and some other city whose name I can't pronounce. Passengers should have their boarding passes out and ready. Have a nice day.

(JONAH returns his attention to the people in line ahead of him. AGENT HOOPER, a man in a trench coat and fedora, slowly moves up behind Jonah. When JONAH looks at his watch yet again, HOOPER speaks loudly to him.)

HOOPER: Mr. Jonah, I presume.

(JONAH starts and drops his suitcase. He turns nervously to face Agent Hooper.)

HOOPER *(CONT)*: Agent Hooper with the IRS.

JONAH: I filed on time!

HOOPER: No, no. The other one. The International Reconcilers for Salvation.

JONAH: *(relieved)* Oh. *(then, as it sinks in)* Oooooh.

HOOPER: Mr. Jonah, aren't you in the wrong line?

JONAH: *(increasingly nervous)* No, no, I'm very sure about where I'm going.

(JONAH stuffs his ticket in his pocket. HOOPER pulls a file out of the inside pocket of his trench coat; he flips it open and scans it.)

HOOPER: This plane is going to Tarshish. Our sources indicate that you've been called — or as we refer to it in The Industry, commissioned — by the Lord God Almighty to go to Nineveh. Am I correct?

JONAH: *(looking around nervously)* Oh, that. Yes, of course I'm going to Nineveh. I'm just going there by way of Tarshish. *(HOOPER looks suspicious.)* Urgent family business. *(HOOPER's frown deepens.)* I'm going to see my mother.

HOOPER: *(consulting file)* Our sources indicate that your mother passed away thirteen years ago.

JONAH: *(obviously winging it)* And I still feel the need to visit her tomb, talk to her, take fresh flowers . . .

(JONAH waits hopefully for some indication from Hooper that he's buying this. HOOPER stares back at Jonah impassively.)

HOOPER: So, why are you going to Tarshish?

JONAH: I just told you . . .

HOOPER: Our sources indicate that your mother is buried in this city. About twelve blocks from here.

JONAH: *(losing his cool)* Well maybe your sources are wrong! Ever consider that?

HOOPER: *(with a soothing smile)* Mr. Jonah. Please. Our source is God Almighty. I would hardly suspect God of an error on a matter such as this. Instead, I suspect that you are simply running away from the IRS. Isn't that right, Mr. Jonah?

JONAH: Me? Run away? What a ridiculous thought. Never even occurred to me.

HOOPER: And yet, Mr. Jonah, recently you were heard to say, and I quote *(consulting his file)*, "I'll sleep in the belly of a whale before I step foot in the city of Nineveh." *(looking up)* True?

JONAH: Who on earth told you that? *(HOOPER looks heavenward.)* Oh, all right, maybe. Maybe I said something like that, but . . .

HOOPER: And didn't you book a room at the Squash Blossom Inn in Tarshish for a whole month, beginning tonight?

JONAH: Those are just contingency plans. I mean, I never intended—that is, I figured I could . . .

HOOPER: Save it, Mr. Jonah. Believe me. I've been on the Delinquent Prophet Patrol for a long time, and the stories all boil down to the same thing. Some whiny idealist suddenly decides that being called by the Lord to minister to the heathen is too much like work. Some starry-eyed scholar can't put his words into practice.

JONAH: Now just a minute . . .

FLIGHT ANNOUNCER: *(offstage)* Your attention, please. This is the final boarding call for Flight 1670 to Tarshish. All passengers must report to gate eleven at this time.

JONAH: Look, I'll go to Nineveh. If that's really what you want. But I tell you—they won't listen to me. You can count on that.

HOOPER: Mr. Jonah, as representatives of the International Reconcilers for Salvation, we both know that we must go where we're called. Whether or not the people listen is in God's hands.

JONAH: I know. I know. But just a little job satisfaction . . .

HOOPER: You'll get your reward. *(pointing in the opposite direction)* Shall we?

FLIGHT ANNOUNCER: *(offstage)* Your attention, please. Agent Hooper, please go to a white courtesy phone. You have an urgent message. Agent Hooper, white courtesy phone.

HOOPER: Rats. Mr. Jonah, I'll meet you at gate twenty-four. Go straight there. The flight leaves in half an hour.

(HOOPER rushes off as JONAH waves cheerily.)

JONAH: *(loudly)* No problem. *(after Hooper exits)* In half an hour I'll be halfway to Tarshish!

(JONAH picks up his suitcase and rushes in the opposite direction.)

Don't Worry! God's with Us!

Characters: Robin, Sally, George
Costumes: Contemporary

(ROBIN, a child, sits alone in a pew. After a moment, GEORGE, an adult, enters and sits next to Robin. GEORGE smiles at Robin and pats her on the head. ROBIN smiles back.)

GEORGE: Good morning.

(Without waiting for Robin to respond, GEORGE turns his attention to his worship bulletin. ROBIN watches him with a smile, but GEORGE does not notice. After another few moments SALLY, an adult, enters and sits on the other side of Robin. SALLY smiles at Robin and pats her on the head. ROBIN smiles back. SALLY doesn't notice, looking past Robin to George. As Sally and George talk, ROBIN follows the conversation closely, turning to face the speaker each time.)

SALLY: George! Good morning. Hey, we missed you last week. *(wagging her finger)* Is it trout season already?

GEORGE: I wish. I worked all last weekend. The only fish I saw were the sharks I work with.

SALLY: Well, business must be wonderful if they kept you busy all weekend.

GEORGE: Are you kidding? This recession is killing us. We were trying to come up with 1.5 million in budget cuts — just to keep the doors open.

SALLY: My word! That sounds quite severe.

GEORGE: That's a nice word for it. I tell you, with the increase in foreign competition, problems between labor and management, people spending less, banks loaning less, the Savings and Loan debacle, the deficit — it all looks pretty bleak.

(ROBIN raises her hand as though asking for permission to speak. SALLY and GEORGE, looking over her head, do not notice.)

SALLY: It's frightening, isn't it? Money's tight, jobs are scarce . . . and in the middle of all this, the church leaders suggest that the budget for next year be increased by ten percent. Imagine!

(ROBIN lowers her hand.)

GEORGE: Unbelievable isn't it?

SALLY: What can they be thinking? Attendance hasn't grown. There aren't many new families in town. And most of the families who belong have children who need braces and money for college. The older people are on fixed incomes. Where do they think the money's going to come from? Probably the same place the government thinks taxes should come from — us lucky folks in the middle class. Like we have anything left to give.

GEORGE: I'm all for charitable giving, but I've got real bills to pay first. The niceties will have to wait.

(ROBIN raises her hand again. Again, GEORGE and SALLY do not notice.)

SALLY: Besides, there are bigger problems in the world to worry about — like drugs. Did you hear they arrested some kids at the high school last week for selling crack? The kids from this church go to that high school!

GEORGE: Drugs are only part of it. Teenagers are carrying weapons to school, shooting each other in the parking lot, stabbing their teachers . . . This is the future of America? This is our bright and shining hope?

(ROBIN lowers her hand.)

SALLY: I don't think there is any hope for our society. I'm tempted to just lock my door and stay inside, but we aren't even safe in our own homes anymore. The world is too messed up. We should just blow the place up and start over from scratch.

GEORGE: You got it. I tell you, I'm glad I'm not a kid anymore. At least when we were growing up, we had something to look forward to. These days what can kids expect? Pollution. Disease. The greenhouse effect, nuclear accidents, and a world full of war. Good luck to 'em.

SALLY: Amen to that.

(SALLY and GEORGE settle back and turn their attention to their bulletins. ROBIN starts to raise her hand again, then stops. ROBIN carefully looks at each of them, but they still don't pay attention. ROBIN clears her throat. No reaction.)

ROBIN: Emmanuel.

(SALLY and GEORGE quickly look up, but look at each other.)

SALLY: Did you say something?

GEORGE: No, I thought you . . .

ROBIN: Emmanuel.

(SALLY and GEORGE look at Robin in surprise, then exchange a knowing smile. SALLY leans close to Robin.)

SALLY: Was there something you wanted to say, sweetheart?

ROBIN: I said it. Emmanuel. It means "God with us."

SALLY: *(glancing again at George)* How nice.

ROBIN: It is nice. It's wonderful. We don't have to worry. God is with us.

(SALLY pats Robin on the head and rolls her eyes at George. GEORGE returns the look.)

SALLY AND GEORGE: Kids!

(SALLY and GEORGE settle back and return their attention to their bulletins. ROBIN stands and quietly begins to sing "O Come, O Come, Emmanuel" [soft accompaniment may be provided as needed]. After a moment SALLY and GEORGE stand, one at a time, and join with Robin to complete the first verse of the hymn.)

Loving Billy Montgomery

Characters: Dad, Danny
Costumes: Contemporary

(DAD sits in a chair; he is reading a newspaper. DANNY enters carrying his schoolbooks. He has a black eye and has been roughed up. DAD does not lower his paper when Danny enters.)

DANNY: Hi, Dad. I'm home.

DAD: Hey, Danny. How was school, pal?

DANNY: It made quite an impression on me.

DAD: Fine. It's important to keep your eyes open and take in the world around you.

DANNY: *(touching his eye gingerly)* That might be tough for a couple of days.

DAD: *(lowering newspaper)* What does . . . *(stops as he sees Danny's eye)* Danny, what happened?

DANNY: I didn't duck.

DAD: Were you in a fight?

DANNY: Not exactly. Do you remember the pastor's sermon last Sunday on "turning the other cheek"?

DAD: Of course.

DANNY: Well, I turned the other cheek, but he aimed a little higher than my cheek.

DAD: Who did this to you?

DANNY: Billy Montgomery. He sits behind me.

DAD: Why on earth did Billy hit you?

DANNY: Billy said I was trying to put the moves on Laura Van Peelstine and he didn't like it.

DAD: Is Laura his girlfriend?

DANNY: He thinks so, but everyone knows better. Billy has a crush on her, but Laura can't stand him. She says it makes her break out in hives just to look at him. But even though everyone knows Laura doesn't like Billy, everyone wants to stay on Billy's good side. So most kids stay away from Laura when Billy's around.

DAD: And you didn't stay away from Laura.

DANNY: I couldn't. Mr. Dorminey made her my new lab partner in science class. We had to work together on the same frog the whole period. After school Billy grabbed me and said, "I saw you trying to move in on my girl, Danny. Put up your dukes." So I said, "My pastor said that if someone hits you, turn around so he can hit the other side also."

DAD: And that's when he hit you?

DANNY: No, he said, "I don't go to church." And then he hit me.

DAD: This is inexcusable. You conducted yourself like a gentleman and a Christian, and he was just a plain bully. I'm going to call Billy Montgomery's parents and discuss this problem with them.

DANNY: No, Dad! Don't do that.

DAD: We have to do something.

DANNY: Please let me handle it.

DAD: Another fight is not the answer, son.

DANNY: I'm not talking about fighting. I'm talking about loving Billy Montgomery.

DAD: Bullies don't understand love, Danny. You've got to speak his language.

DANNY: But, Dad, doesn't the Bible say to love your enemies? Maybe Billy doesn't understand love because he hasn't seen enough of it. If I try to show love to Billy instead of fighting back, maybe he'll get the hang of it. Maybe he'll start to understand love.

DAD: Son, I'm very proud of you. You've obviously been listening in church and Sunday school, but what Jesus was really saying when he said to turn the other cheek . . . *(faltering)* I mean, let's examine the cultural context in which the message . . . *(trying again)* Actually, let's just look at this in a practical . . .

(DAD stops, thinks for a moment, then puts his arm around Danny's shoulders.)

DAD *(CONT)*: You're right, Danny. As much as I'd like to be the one punching Billy Montgomery right now, as much as I want to chew his folks out, what you're saying is right. We must love our enemies.

DANNY: It's hard to remember that some times, isn't it, Dad?

DAD: Yes, Danny, it is. Maybe none of us understand love as much as we should. Maybe we all need our eyes opened. But first, let's get some ice on that eye of yours.

DANNY: Oh, it doesn't hurt all that much, Dad. But I do have one question. When Jesus said we should turn the other cheek, did he say anything about still keeping your eye on the other guy?

DAD: You know, Danny, I bet there's even a verse that tells us ducking is not a sin.

(DAD and DANNY exit together.)

The Weight Loss

Characters: Mr. Perkins, Roberta, James, Linda, Group Members
Costumes: Contemporary

(The meeting room of a weight-loss group. A scale is center, surrounded by a circle of chairs. Some members of the group are seated, some are mingling and chatting. MR. PERKINS enters, clipboard in hand. People react with excitement to his entrance.)

PERKINS: Okay, folks! Let's take our seats and get started! *(as people sit down)* Welcome to the monthly meeting of Weight Tossers, Chapter 693. I'm Mr. Perkins, the chapter tossmaster. Let's begin as we do every meeting by reciting our "pledge of a lossness."

(ALL leap to their feet and stand with their right hands over their stomachs.)

ALL: We pledge to lose by making fatty foods our taboos, for it's pounds we must toss if we want some hefty weight loss. DON'T EAT IT!

(They cheer and applaud each other and sit back down. PERKINS remains standing.)

PERKINS: Great! Now, this will probably be a difficult meeting for many of us, since we've just come through the holidays. Please don't feel bad if you tip the scale a little more tonight than you expect to. The holidays are full of temptation, and we're all bound to slip a bit. But we'll get back on track in no time, so let's stay positive. Still, I am going to give you each the option of weighing yourself privately tonight and keeping the results to yourself. After all, you're doing this for yourselves, not for anyone else, and your progress is your business. It's between you and the scale. Okay? So . . . anyone want to start?

(ROBERTA leaps to her feet, waving her hand enthusiastically.)

ROBERTA: Oh, Mr. Perkins! I'm not ashamed of my weight. In fact, the more people who know of my incredible self-discipline and the resulting extraordinary loss of pounds, the better I feel.

PERKINS: Okay, Roberta. Step on up.

(ROBERTA primps, making sure all eyes are on her, then steps up on the scale. PERKINS adjusts the scale.)

ROBERTA: Get ready for the good news of great joy!

PERKINS: 114 pounds. Let's see, that's . . .

ROBERTA: *(waving her arms in jubilation)* Seven pounds LESS than last month! I know it's unbelievable, but, trust me, it was a piece of cake. Low-cal cake, that is!

PERKINS: Truly a good month, Roberta.

ROBERTA: And it's all because of that special talent God has given me: self-discipline. Let's be honest! Very few people have it. But I do. What a blessing!

PERKINS: Thanks for sharing those impressive words, Roberta.

(PERKINS pulls her off the scale and guides her back to her seat. The others applaud. PERKINS barely has Roberta back in her seat when JAMES leaps up.)

JAMES: I'll go next, Mr. Perkins.

PERKINS: Okay, James. Come on up.

(JAMES races up onto the scale. He can barely stand still while PERKINS adjusts the scale.)

JAMES: I too have been detouring the donuts.

PERKINS: And you've lost six pounds.

JAMES: Yes! Six wonderful, fatty-tissued pounds shed from this fit and trim body.

PERKINS: Congratulations, James.

JAMES: *(with growing exuberance and volume)* Six pounds of extra weight caused by addiction to chocolate-covered donuts and cream-filled eclairs!

PERKINS: *(trying to guide him off the scale)* Thank you for sharing . . .

JAMES: Six pounds of needless, excess cargo that has now been flushed from the vessel . . .

PERKINS: Okay, James!

(JAMES stops, startled, and returns to his seat, not sure what Perkins' problem is.)

PERKINS *(CONT)*: Anyone else? *(No one responds.)* All right, then it's time for the Weight Tossers to head down the hall for tonight's educational film. It's about the effects on the human body of Hershey's Chocolate Kisses when eaten right before bedtime. It's called "The Kisses of Death." Let's go see it and learn.

(Everyone files out but LINDA, who stays in her seat until the others are gone. When she is alone, she stands and walks slowly to the scale.)

LINDA: "But when you pray, do not be like the hypocrites, for they love to pray standing in the synagogues and on the street corners to be seen by men. I tell you the truth, they have received their reward in full. When you pray, go into your room, close the door and pray to your Father, who is unseen."[2]

(LINDA steps on the scale, adjusts it, and gives a victory jab in the air when she sees the results.)

LINDA: Yes!

(LINDA blows a kiss upward and races out after the others.)

---

[2]Matthew 6:5-6

Be Reasonable

Characters: Roger, Craig, Jean, Tom, Barbara
Costumes: Contemporary

(A meeting of the church leaders. ROGER, CRAIG, JEAN, TOM, and BARBARA are gathered around the conference table in the meeting room.)

ROGER: Okay, next is the Mission Committee report. Craig, what do you have for us tonight?

CRAIG: Well, Roger, our next project is the Christ for the World Offering. The committee has been discussing a target goal for the congregation's offering, and we've decided that two thousand dollars is not unreasonable.

(There are murmurs all around the table.)

ROGER: Well. Two thousand dollars. That's quite . . . admirable.

JEAN: Admirable? It's insane. How does the Mission Committee expect us to come up with that kind of an offering?

TOM: I agree, Jean. We're already having budget problems here in our own congregation, and you think we're going to give that kind of money to an outside group?

ROGER: They aren't an outside group, Tom. They're part of our church.

BARBARA: But you're still talking about a special offering program, and those always take away from giving to the General Fund. The budget can't handle that.

CRAIG: I understand your concern, Barbara, but the missionaries are having budget problems, too. Things are tough all over—all over the world. But the missionaries still have work to do, work that deserves our support. We're not asking that much of the members. Two thousand dollars works out to just $3.57 per member.

JEAN: Craig, be reasonable.

CRAIG: I thought I was! What do you consider reasonable?

TOM: Three hundred dollars, tops.

CRAIG: Three hundred dollars! Are you kidding? Do you know how many patients were treated last year at the two hospitals we support in India? One hundred and seventy-two thousand! And that's just one program! There are so many people who need our help. Two thousand dollars is only a drop in the bucket, and you say it's too much?

BARBARA: All right, Craig. Quit with the guilt-trip stuff. It's not going to work. We have problems right here at home we should be attending to, and you aren't going to get us sidetracked on all this foreign jazz.

CRAIG: This foreign jazz is people, Barbara. Not just the people our missionaries help, but the missionaries themselves—who went overseas backed by our promise to support them and their work. We promised to feed and clothe them. How can we turn our backs on them now?

ROGER: Craig, we admire your passion, but don't let it blind you to the reality of the situation. We've examined the issue: We can't support your recommendation of a two-thousand-dollar offering. Therefore, I move that we consider the three-hundred-dollar figure that was mentioned.

TOM: I second the motion.

CRAIG: Wait . . .

ROGER: All in favor?

TOM, BARBARA, AND JEAN: Aye.

ROGER: All opposed?

CRAIG: Nay! Nay!

ROGER: Majority rules, Craig. Now, let's move on to Tom and his important news.

TOM: Thank you, Roger. Folks, on behalf of the Finance Committee, it's my privilege to present something truly exciting. We've been working on this for months, and it's finally becoming a reality.

(TOM stands and unrolls a large blueprint, which he holds open for all to see.)

TOM *(CONT)*: Here are the plans for our church's very own, state-of-the-art gymnasium.

(ROGER, BARBARA, and JEAN crowd around in excitement. CRAIG drops his head into his hands in disbelief.)

What Shall I Wear?

Characters: Aggie, Brenda
Costumes: Contemporary

(AGGIE and BRENDA enter a clothing store. BRENDA immediately goes to a rack of dresses and flips through them, agitated.)

BRENDA: I'll never find the right thing to wear to the big youth conference next weekend. I know it.

AGGIE: Brenda, you're way too worried about what you're going to wear. It's no big deal. It doesn't matter to him.

BRENDA: Aggie! Of course it matters! Pastor Jones said last week that whenever even two or three people gather together because of Jesus, he's there with them. Several hundred people will be there Saturday, so Jesus is bound to be there, right? And he's a king, right? We're talking royalty here. You know, Prince of Peace, King of kings, Lord of lords.

AGGIE: And all around cool guy. You're stressing for no reason, Brenda.

(BRENDA grabs a dress off the rack and holds it up in front of her.)

BRENDA: What about this? It's nice and summery.

AGGIE: It's not your color.

BRENDA: *(slamming the dress back on the rack)* You're so much help, Aggie.

AGGIE: Brenda, what you wear doesn't matter to him. Jesus has never been impressed by a person's clothes. They aren't important to him, and they shouldn't be so important to you.

BRENDA: I see what you're saying. I should go casual. Jeans, maybe. *(moving to another rack)* Acid wash, prewashed, stonewash. Faded, torn, shredded. Which do you think he'd go for?

AGGIE: Brenda, listen to me! It does not matter! You could show up in a potato sack, and it wouldn't make any difference to him.

BRENDA: How can you say that, Aggie? This is the most important person I will ever meet. I have to look perfect. Remember when my dad got us box seats for the Bon Jovi concert? I spent three weeks looking for the perfect outfit to wear, even though I figured we'd never get within twenty feet of Jon. But it was important that I look hot in his honor. And now, we're talking about meeting a king and you're acting like we could go in our pajamas and no one would bat an eye.

AGGIE: He said it himself, Brenda. He said, and I quote, "Therefore I tell you, do not worry about your life, what you will eat or drink; or about your body, what you will wear. Is not life more important than food, and the body more important than clothes?"[3]

(BRENDA considers this a moment, then shrugs.)

BRENDA: You're taking it out of context.

AGGIE: I am not!

BRENDA: Okay, then why do people say things like, "What a heavenly outfit" or "You look like an angel"? Hmmmm? Why do people talk about something gorgeous being "out of this world"? Hmmmm? Come on, Miss Answer Person. Explain that.

AGGIE: Those are words, Brenda. Most of the people who use them have no idea what they truly mean. They don't stop to think. They just look and evaluate. The surface is all

---

[3]Matthew 6:25

that matters to them. Don't you understand? That's exactly why Jesus doesn't care what you wear. The surface doesn't matter to him. What's underneath—what's inside—is what he cares about.

BRENDA: Honest? I could be months out of style, and he wouldn't care? I could have a major geek haircut, and he'd like me anyway?

AGGIE: Better than that. He'd love you.

BRENDA: Wow. So what do you think I should wear?

AGGIE: Exactly what you have on.

BRENDA: This old thing?

AGGIE: Yes! It looks fine. It looks like you.

BRENDA: Well . . . Okay. But it's not my best color.

(AGGIE rolls her eyes and they start to exit.)

BRENDA *(CONT)*: Maybe we should stop off at the salon and get our nails done at least.

AGGIE: Brenda!

BRENDA: Just checking . . .

(They exit.)

Joy and Roy

Characters: Joy, Roy
Costumes: Contemporary

(Roy enters a bus and sits down in a seat. He puts his duffel bag at his feet and looks out the window.)

Roy: What a great retreat! Not even this long bus ride home will spoil my fantastic spiritual high!

(Joy enters the bus. Roy doesn't notice her. Joy surveys the whole bus, but the only seat is the one next to Roy. Joy looks at him with distaste.)

Joy: Oh, great. One empty seat on the whole bus, and it has to be next to this guy.

(Reluctantly, Joy sits next to Roy. Roy glances at her as she puts her overnight bag at her feet.)

Roy: *(sarcastic)* Terrific. I get to sit next to some girl who thinks she's God's gift to men.

Joy: Here I am, going back to my beautiful Christian college, and I get stuck next to this guy. What a bum. Probably hooked on drugs.

Roy: She's probably so hooked on herself that no one else exists. I bet her bedroom is nothing but mirrors, so she can adore herself all the time.

Joy: Why do people get mixed up with drugs anyway? What a waste.

Roy: Why do people like this even exist? What could God possibly have in mind for them?

Joy: He's going to offer me drugs. Probably has cocaine in his pocket and something worse in his bag.

Roy: Her bag is probably full of eighteen different colors of makeup. I'm going to have to sit here and watch her paint her face the whole trip.

Joy: It's too bad this guy doesn't know what life is all about.

Roy: It's too bad this girl doesn't know what life is all about.

Joy: One great thing about being a Christian, you really begin to appreciate who you are — as opposed to who you might have been. Like this stoner here.

Roy: One great thing about being a Christian, you really being to appreciate who you are — as opposed to who you'd like to be. Like Miss Magazine Cover here.

Joy: The more I'm around people like this dopehead, the more I value my Christian friends. It's so good to be able to talk about Jesus with other believers.

Roy: This girl is such a turnoff. Man, I'm glad I have my Christian friends, so I can talk openly about how the Spirit has turned me on and turned my life around.

Joy: He keeps looking at me. He wants to talk. I'll get my Bible out and read it. That'll scare him away.

Roy: She keeps looking at me. She's flirting. I'll get my Bible out and read it. That'll show her I'm not interested in her kind.

(Joy and Roy reach into their bags at the same time. Startled, they look at each other and pause a moment. Then, they both pull out their Bibles with a flourish, making sure the other notices. Each realizes what the other is holding, and they look at each other in amazement.)

Joy: You have . . .

Roy: You read . . .

Joy: Are you a Christian?

Roy: You bet! And you?

Joy: I sure am. You know, I picked you out right away. The minute I got on the bus, I said to myself, "I bet he's a Christian."

Roy: Amazing. I was thinking the exact same thing about you.

(Joy and Roy shake hands.)

Removing the Shaving Cream

Characters: Ted, Fred, Rhonda, Carl
Costumes: Contemporary

(FRED is mowing his front lawn. TED enters and waves. FRED shuts off the mower and goes to greet Ted. Both men sport beards of shaving cream, but neither one seems to notice.)

FRED: Hey, neighbor. Welcome home. How was the reunion?

TED: Wonderful, but it's nice to be home. Did I miss anything in church yesterday?

FRED: A good sermon. Some fine hymns. And my personal revelation. Ted, the Lord has given me a great gift. In the last few months, the faults of other people have been becoming so clear to me; it's as though I can see it on their faces. I realized yesterday that the Lord is giving me eyes that can see the imperfections of others.

TED: Me, too! I've been experiencing the exact same thing. It must be a sign of our advanced spiritual growth that we're able to look at people and, within a few minutes, tell where they have fallen short.

FRED: Precisely. Yesterday I was able to identify eight people within our congregation that the pastor's sermon was really hitting.

TED: Fabulous.

FRED: It was a message about commitment to the Lord, and I could go right around the sanctuary and tell you by name the folks who aren't truly committed.

TED: Fred, the Lord may be calling you to a new ministry of loving criticism.

FRED: Even insightful judgment!

TED: Amen!!

FRED: I've always believed that the church would be so much better if spiritual people like you and me — people with vision — could be permitted to point out the shortcomings of others.

TED: Wouldn't that be wonderful!

FRED: Once we've pointed out the shortcomings, it's not much more work to tell them exactly what they need to do to fix things up and live up to our standards.

TED: I agree with you 100 percent.

FRED: Don't you think that it would actually attract people to the church?

TED: A swift path to perfection? No question about it.

FRED: People could see how great those who attend our church have become. They would be drawn to us because they would want to experience that efficiency and perfection.

TED: But it can't happen until we're able to point out to all those around us the various ways in which they fall short.

FRED: Speaking of falling short, look who's coming. Rhonda. The gal with the hideous blemish on her nose.

TED: I wonder if she knows how ridiculous she looks.

FRED: Obviously not, or she would have done something about it.

(RHONDA enters, walking down the sidewalk in front of Fred's house. She has a tiny dab of shaving cream on the tip of her nose.)

TED: How can she not see it, when it's so obvious — and so ugly — to the rest of us?

FRED: We should tell her.

(TED looks at Fred nervously, thinking it over.)

TED: You're right. Maybe this could be the correction that helps her get her life back on track.

FRED: My thoughts exactly.

Ted: Rhonda! Rhonda, hello!

(Rhonda stops and waves. Ted and Fred hurry across the lawn to her.)

Rhonda: Hello, Ted, Fred. Good to see you.

Ted: Rhonda, we're so glad you happened by. There's something we've been meaning to talk to you about. We feel it is our sacred obligation to inform you, since you obviously can't see it for yourself.

Rhonda: Ted, what are you talking about?

Fred: It's your nose, Rhonda. Don't you know you have something on your nose? It's plain as day. Don't you ever look in the mirror?

Ted: Please understand that we're telling you this in your own best interest. We want to help you get your act together. I mean, we don't have to offer this loving criticism. But we want to.

Rhonda: You two ought to mind your own business and take care of your own problems.

(Rhonda hurries away, stopping to collect herself some distance from the two men. Ted and Fred look after her, perplexed.)

Fred: The truth is hard for some people.

Ted: Imagine. Trying to tell us that we have problems. Just trying to distract us from her problem I suppose.

Fred: This is a greater task than we had imagined, my friend. We'll have to have a plan. Why don't you come in for a glass of iced tea? We'll begin by making a list of the people who most desperately need our help.

(Fred and Ted exit. Carl enters and walks quickly to Rhonda.)

Carl: Ma'am, are you all right?

Rhonda: *(defensive)* Why do you ask?

Carl: I saw you talking to those men, and they seemed to upset you.

Rhonda: They're just stupid jerks. Who cares what they say?

Carl: Actually, I think I know what they were trying to do. They simply went about it the wrong way.

Rhonda: What do you mean?

Carl: *(taking out a handkerchief)* You have a small spot of shaving cream on the end of your nose. I believe they wanted to help you remove it. Here. Use my handkerchief.

(Rhonda takes the handkerchief and wipes her nose.)

Rhonda: I'm so embarrassed.

Carl: No need to be. I had the same problem myself last week, but fortunately my neighbor offered me his handkerchief, not a lot of harsh words.

Rhonda: You were very lucky. Now, so am I.

Carl: I was walking down to the corner café for some lunch. Care to join me?

Rhonda: Thank you. *(as they being to exit)* Oh, here's your handkerchief.

Carl: Please. You keep it. A neighbor of yours may need it. Pass it along.

(They exit.)

Stone Bread

Characters: Gordie, Henry
Costumes: Contemporary

(It's lunchtime in the school cafeteria. GORDIE sits at a table, spreading his lunch out around him. HENRY enters with his lunchbox and sits next to Gordie.)

GORDIE: Yo, Henry. What's happenin'?

HENRY: Not a whole lot, Gordie. What's for lunch today?

GORDIE: Hey, man, my mom did it up right today. Check this. *(pointing)* She started me out with my all-time favorite.

HENRY: Whoa. Celery sticks stuffed with chunky peanut butter. You must have done something awesome to deserve that.

GORDIE: Nope, just did what I'm supposed to do—fed the dog, took out the trash. As long as I don't feed the trash and throw out the dog, I'm cool.

HENRY: So what else did you get?

GORDIE: *(doing a drum roll on the table)* Pimento cheese sandwiches.

HENRY: Righteous!

GORDIE: And a bag of pretzels, a juicy orange, and—to top it all off—chocolate Ho Hos.

HENRY: Gordie, you cleaned up big time.

GORDIE: And how do you plan to chow down, Henry?

HENRY: I haven't even looked.

(HENRY opens his lunchbox and stares at the contents for a moment. His expression becomes one of puzzlement, then of anger.)

HENRY *(CONT)*: What's going on here?

(HENRY takes a stone out of his lunchbox and holds it up for Gordie to see.)

GORDIE: Strange-looking lunch, Henry.

HENRY: My mom packed me a rock!

GORDIE: She must think you aren't getting enough minerals.

(GORDIE laughs at his own joke. HENRY is not amused.)

HENRY: My own mother packed me a rock for my lunch!

GORDIE: Well, Henry, she did butter the top for you. *(reaching into Henry's lunchbox)* And here's a knife to slice it with and some baloney to slide on in there once it's sliced. Yum, yum.

HENRY: *(rapping the rock on the table)* Gordie, this is a rock. The knife will not cut a rock.

GORDIE: Right. *(beat)* Henry, this isn't want you asked to have for lunch today, is it?

HENRY: Of course not. I asked for turkey on wheat with lettuce and mayo.

GORDIE: *(thoughtfully)* I think it's safe to say that your mom blew it.

HENRY: What's she trying to tell me? What did I do to her?

GORDIE: Hey, don't take it personally, Henry. Maybe your mom just had a bad morning.

(HENRY turns and faces the audience, holding the stone up for all to see.)

HENRY: "Which of you, if his son asks for bread, will give him a stone? . . . If you, then, though you are evil, know how to give good gifts to your children, how much more will your Father in heaven give good gifts to those who ask him!"[4]

(HENRY sits heavily and contemplates his stone.)

GORDIE: Hey, Henry. Want a Ho Ho?

---

[4]Matthew 7:9

Real Estate Crashes

Characters: Mick, Mary
Costumes: Contemporary

(MICK races into his office and looks around in despair. MARY hurries in behind him. MICK thrashes around in the papers on his desk, then throws them up in the air in frustration. MARY watches with a worried frown.)

MICK: I'm ruined! Totally ruined! Completely and utterly destroyed! I can't believe this is happening.

MARY: Now, Mick, it's not all that bad.

MICK: *(pointing)* Mary, look out that window and tell me what you see.

(MARY walks reluctantly to the window. She already knows what's out there, and she's not eager to look again. MICK gestures impatiently until she looks. When she speaks, MARY does her best to be upbeat.)

MARY: Ahhhh. Well . . . I see . . . water.

MICK: Water! You see water, do you? Just "water"?

MARY: Uhhhhh . . . Okay. I guess . . . well, I guess it's a swiftly flowing body of water. I guess you might even call it a river.

MICK: *(nearing apoplexy)* And what do you suppose is in that river?

MARY: *(with a shrug)* Water. Sediment. Plant life. Are there fish around here?

MICK: *(explosive)* Mary! *(trying to contain himself)* I mean, what do you suppose those are floating there on top of the river?

MARY: *(pretending to be surprised)* Oh, those. Why, those look like mobile homes.

MICK: And why do you suppose those mobile homes are floating in the river, Mary?

(MARY takes a deep breath and goes for broke.)

MARY: Because they used to be in the Desert Sands Trailer Park. Before the rain started. And the dam broke. And the old riverbed filled back up and washed them all away. *(gesturing)* Just swept 'em right out of there. Right off that land. Of which you are the sole owner. And therefore, for which you are completely liable.

MICK: *(sinking into his chair)* This is a catastrophe! The end of the world! What am I going to do?

MARY: Guess it's kinda late to get flood insurance.

MICK: *(pounding his desk)* Why didn't I listen to my father?

MARY: You mean, when he told you to put the trailer park up there on that piece of high ground—way above the old riverbed? *(pointing out the window)* Gee. Sure looks nice and dry up there. Bet your father would've gotten you a good price, too.

MICK: Oh, Mary, why didn't I buy that piece of high ground instead of *(gesturing)* the Desert Sands River Valley out there?

MARY: *(another deep breath)* Well, I would have to say that it's because you're a cheapskate and a tightwad. But it seems to me that you explained it all a little differently. Something about financial feasibility, buy low and sell high, I can do it without my dad, that sort of thing.

MICK: No, no, you're right! Absolutely right! I was cheap and proud. And now I'm ruined. I had to go for the quick buck, never mind the consequences, and look where it got me.

MARY: Guess your quick bucks are now quicksand.

(MARY laughs in delight. MICK glares at her until she stops.)
MICK: Come on. Let's see if there's anything worth saving.
(MICK stomps out. MARY hurries after him. As they go, MARY continues.)
MARY: Look at the bright side, Mick. You've been talking about investing in waterfront prop-
erty . . .

Honus Wagner

Characters: Mrs. Martin, Ernie, Narrator
Costumes: Contemporary

(Ernie sits in a comfortable living room, flipping through a stack of baseball cards. He wears the cap of his favorite baseball team. Mrs. Martin, an elderly woman, enters with another box of baseball cards.)

Mrs. Martin: I found one more box, Ernie. It was stuck back in one corner of the attic, behind the old Philco—the first radio Mr. Martin and I ever had.

Ernie: *(taking the box from her)* Thank you, Mrs. Martin. Mr. Martin sure had a great collection. There are some amazing cards here—a 1963 Mickey Mantle, a '56 Stan Musial, Sandy Koufax's rookie card. All the top players from back then.

Mrs. Martin: Really! I'm afraid I never followed baseball. Roy was the fan in this family. He spent the entire season with one ear to the radio and one eye on the box scores in the paper.

Ernie: He sure took good care of his cards. Most of these are in excellent condition.

Mrs. Martin: I suppose that's important to a collector like you.

Ernie: Oh, yes, ma'am. Baseball cards are like antiques. Each year they appreciate—even more so if they're in good condition.

Mrs. Martin: I always thought it was just a harmless hobby of Roy's. It gave him pleasure, and I didn't think anything else of it.

Ernie: Let's check out this box. *(flipping through)* Wow. These cards are even older. *(flipping more, growing excited)* Lou Boudreau! Dizzy Dean! Whoa! Lou Gehrig!

Mrs. Martin: There's a name I remember.

(Ernie freezes, eyes fixed on one card. After a moment he leaps to his feet, his excitement so intense that he can barely speak.)

Ernie: Honus Wagner! HONUS WAGNER!! *(almost hyperventilating)* HO-NUS WAGNER!!! *(shaking the card at her)* Honus . . .

Mrs. Martin: Was he a favorite of yours, Ernie?

Ernie: A favorite? Mrs. Martin, I have dreamed of this card. This is . . . I mean, it's a real-life, honest-to-goodness Honus Wagner. And it's in mint condition. Mint! Absolutely beautiful.

Mrs. Martin: And the mint condition enhances its value, right?

Ernie: *(trying to collect himself)* Mrs. Martin, this card is incredibly rare. For it to be mint . . . This card has to be worth . . .

Mrs. Martin: Let me guess. Forty dollars?

Ernie: Oh, man. Try forty thousand dollars.

Mrs. Martin: *(disbelieving)* For a baseball card?

Ernie: I could be wrong. It could be worth even more. It's been a long time since I've heard of one on the market.

Mrs. Martin: Well, I never. And it's just been sitting up there gathering dust.

Ernie: Mrs. Martin, I want to buy this from you. How much would you like for it?

Mrs. Martin: Oh, Ernie. We've already established that I don't know much about these cards. I couldn't possibly tell you a fair price . . .

Ernie: Forty thousand dollars? Fifty thousand dollars?

Mrs. Martin: Ernie, I didn't even pay that for this house. I have no idea . . .

Ernie: Name your price, Mrs. Martin, and I'll pay it. I have to have this card. It'll be the centerpiece of my entire collection. It's perfect. I can't miss this chance.

Mrs. Martin: But Ernie, you're talking about so much money . . .

Ernie: I'll sell my car, my house . . . whatever it takes.

Mrs. Martin: You would sell all your possessions just to have this card?

Ernie: I'll get a loan. I'll get a second job. I'll eat peanut butter and jelly 'til doomsday. I must have this card.

Mrs. Martin: I tell you what. You pay me what you can afford and it's yours.

Ernie: *(literally jumping for joy)* Yes! Yes! A mint Honus Wagner and it's mine! Thank you! Thank you! This is the happiest day of my life.

Mrs. Martin: Let's hope you still feel that way ten years from now.

Ernie: Oh, I will . . . even if I'm still making payments to you, I will. Mrs. Martin, this is wonderful. Thank you. I'll start paying you as soon as I can. I don't know how to thank you enough.

Mrs. Martin: Seeing your joy is thanks enough, Ernie.

(Ernie lets out a whoop of joy and races out. Mrs. Martin watches after him with a smile.)

Mrs. Martin: A tiny little piece of cardboard. Roy, if I had only known. Makes me wonder how someone might feel about the old Philco.

(As Mrs. Martin exits:)

Narrator: "The kingdom of heaven is like treasure hidden in a field. When a man found it, he hid it again, and then in his joy went and sold all he had and bought that field. Again, the kingdom of heaven is like a merchant looking for fine pearls. When he found one of great value, he went away and sold everything he had and bought it."[5]

---

[5]Matthew 13:44-46

The FRQ

Characters: Lisa, Dave
Costumes: Contemporary

(Lisa sits at the kitchen table, working out a problem on a calculator. Dave enters, removing his coat as he approaches Lisa.)

Dave: Hi, sweetheart! Sorry I'm late.

(Dave kisses her on top of the head. Lisa does not react, attention riveted on the calculator.)

Dave *(cont)*: Lisa? Honey? What are you doing?

Lisa: *(not looking up)* Figuring up my Forgiveness Reserve Quantity.

Dave: Say what?

Lisa: My FRQ. Forgiveness Reserve Quantity.

Dave: Does this have something to do with conserving energy? saving water?

Lisa: It may have to do with conserving the energy you expend getting yourself into hot water.

Dave: I'm not sure I follow.

Lisa: I'm figuring my FRQ as it relates to your coming home late. According to my calculations, tonight makes the 311th time you've been late in the last twenty-two months and fifteen days. That means your Forgiveness Reserve Quantity is down to 179. If my figures are correct and you continue in your present pattern of lateness, you'll have exhausted my FRQ by next April thirtieth.

Dave: What happens then?

Lisa: Well, as I interpret Scripture, I will be justified at that time to have you flogged in the town square, tarred and feathered, and then deprived of the TV remote control for the entire football season.

Dave: This is starting to sound serious. C'mon, hon, we've been over this dozens of times. You know I try to get home on time, but sometimes my appointments run late. Like last Tuesday. I was on schedule until Mr. Brown started asking me about insurance for his cat in addition to the life insurance he was buying for himself.

Lisa: Last Tuesday?

Dave: It was a memorable argument once I got home, Lisa. You must remember.

Lisa: Actually, I almost forgot. *(punching numbers into calculator)* That means your true FRQ is 178 and D-day is April twenty-eighth.

Dave: Where did you come up with all this?

Lisa: It's in the Bible, Dave. Jesus said, "Don't just forgive your husband for being late seven times. Give him 490 chances."

Dave: Are you sure you've got that quote right?

Lisa: More or less. Jesus said to forgive people seven times seventy.

Dave: Where does he discuss keeping a countdown chart?

Lisa: How else do you expect me to know when you've used up your absolutions?

Dave: That's not what Jesus meant, Lisa.

Lisa: Oh? I suppose he told you something he didn't tell the rest of us? Come on, Dave! If Jesus himself had an appointment with you, you'd keep him waiting.

Dave: I'm not saying I have different information—just a different perspective.

Lisa: I bet you do. I should have known from the very beginning—when you were a half an hour late for our wedding!

Dave: I've apologized for that one a fair number of times, Lisa. I took a wrong turn, okay?

Lisa: The church was across the street from your house!

DAVE: I was nervous!

LISA: Well, no need to be nervous now. I won't zap you until you're late the 491st time.

DAVE: Lisa, please. I admit that being late is one of my weaknesses; I truly am sorry, and I am trying to be better about it. But when Jesus said seven times seventy, he wasn't saying we should set a limit. He meant we should go beyond our limits, we should forgive more than we would think of forgiving.

LISA: I think 490 times is more than most people would forgive.

DAVE: What about all the times we fail God? Do you think God should zap us when we hit 490?

LISA: That certainly is God's right.

DAVE: But God doesn't do it, Lisa. God even allowed his Son to die for us, even though we passed the 490 mark a long, long time ago.

LISA: *(after a moment)* You're right. I hate it when that happens.

DAVE: And I hate it when I upset you. I'm sorry I was late — again.

LISA: *(shrugging, pushing the calculator away)* That's okay. I suppose if you can forgive me, I can forgive you.

DAVE: Oh, sweetheart, why do I need to forgive you?

LISA: My mother called today. She's coming for a two-week visit.

DAVE: Two weeks? Here? When?

LISA: *(looking at her watch)* Oh, about an hour from now . . . unless she's late . . .

Labor Agreements

Characters: Joe, Kyle, Pat, Kelly, Mr. Shepherd
Costumes: Contemporary

(JOE, KYLE, PAT, and KELLY are dressed in work clothes and sit around a conference table. They all look quite unhappy.)

JOE: We can't let him get away with this. If not for our own sake, then for the sake of our fellow workers. If we let this happen, who knows what we'll have to compromise on next!

KYLE: I'm with you, Joe. The guy is trying to push us back twenty years.

KELLY: It's causing a lot of dissension on the floor, that's for sure.

PAT: And why? We give him a good day's work, and this is our thanks? Terrific.

JOE: Quiet. Here he comes.

(MR. SHEPHERD, dressed in a suit, enters. He is humming. When he sees the group, he smiles pleasantly.)

MR. SHEPHERD: Joe. Kyle. Kelly. Pat. Good to see you all.

(MR. SHEPHERD extends his hand. No one takes it. He shrugs, smiles, and sits down.)

JOE: Let's not pretend this is going to be pleasant, Mr. Shepherd. We have a problem.

MR. SHEPHERD: I'm sorry to hear that, Joe. If there's a problem, I certainly want to fix it. What's up?

KYLE: The official term is "unfair labor practices."

MR. SHEPHERD: *(surprised)* Unfair? That's pretty severe, folks.

JOE: We're talking about the new people you've hired in the last thirty days.

MR. SHEPHERD: I haven't heard any complaints. Aren't they doing their work? Do you feel you're having to do more than your share?

KELLY: It's not their work that's the problem, Mr. Shepherd. They're doing a great job. It's the money they're being paid to do that work that gripes us.

MR. SHEPHERD: I'm paying them exactly what I'm paying you.

KYLE: Bingo.

PAT: I've worked for this company for twenty-six years. Joe's been here twenty-seven. Kyle and Kelly have put in twenty-five each.

MR. SHEPHERD: And I'm proud you've stayed with me all this time. I trust you all enjoyed your anniversary bonuses.

(JOE, KYLE, KELLY, and PAT nod and look at each other uneasily.)

PAT: You've been good to us. Fine. That's not our point. What we want to know is . . . what's with these young turks, barely out of the playpen, who come in here and start getting paid the same salary we're making?

KELLY: They aren't even in the union.

KYLE: It's not fair.

MR. SHEPHERD: Let me get this straight. Are you four unhappy with your salaries?

JOE: No, sir. You pay us an equitable wage. Right?

KELLY, KYLE AND PAT: Yes.

JOE: But these new guys! They're getting the same salary—and the same benefits—that we get, and we've been here longer than half of 'em have been walking!

MR. SHEPHERD: But you aren't trying to talk me into giving you a raise.

JOE: No, sir. We're pleased with our compensation.

MR. SHEPHERD: Then, at the risk of sounding rude, there's no need for further discussion. Frankly, it is none of your business what I pay anyone else at this company.

KYLE: We have a stake in this company and the way it's run.

MR. SHEPHERD: And you enjoy the benefits accordingly. Right?

KYLE: Yes, sir, but . . .

MR. SHEPHERD: *(holding up a hand)* Kyle, listen to me. I've treated you well through the years. All of you. If I choose to pay these new people the same wage, you shouldn't complain. You lose nothing by it. I haven't taken anything away from you in order to give to them. This is a healthy, thriving company. There's room for anyone willing to work hard. The deals I strike with these people are confidential — between each employee and me. You each signed a contract with me. They were negotiated in good faith, and I have been faithful to those contracts to the last detail. But it seems to me that we aren't talking about contracts or labor practices or anything of that sort here. We're talking about jealousy, plain and simple. I can't do anything to change that. That's something you have to deal with on your own.

(MR. SHEPHERD stands, looks at the stunned group a moment, and exits. JOE, KELLY, KYLE, and PAT look after him in silence a moment. JOE stands and begins to exit after Mr. Shepherd.)

PAT: Joe, wait! We haven't decided what to do yet!

JOE: What can we do, Pat?

PAT: Uhhh . . . Organize a strike, or a boycott, walk off the job. Maybe write our congressman!

JOE: Why? You heard the man. He pays us fairly. He's upheld his end of the contract. He's right. There's nothing else to talk about. Issue closed.

(JOE exits. KYLE and KELLY slowly rise and start out after Joe.)

PAT: Kyle! Kelly! Let's fight for this!

(KYLE and KELLY look back, shake their heads, and exit. PAT leaps up and pounds the table.)

PAT *(CONT)*: Well, I'm not going to just roll over and play dead for this guy. I mean, who does he think he is? God???

Playing Favorites

Characters: Debbie, Fred, Lucy, Mom
Costumes: Contemporary

(DEBBIE, FRED, and LUCY are sitting in the living room of their mother's house.)
DEBBIE: I still say Fred was the favorite.
FRED: I was not! You have the stupidest ideas, Debbie.
LUCY: He's right, Debbie. You were the one who always got to do exactly what you wanted. Mama's special little girl.
FRED: Slow down, Lucy. If we're putting it to a vote, my vote goes to you.
LUCY: Me?!? Get real.
FRED: It's true. You're the oldest; you got all the attention, all the new clothes and toys. You had Mom all to yourself for almost three years. Debbie and I got your hand-me-downs and Mom's extra few minutes here and there. All the special stuff was always reserved for you.
LUCY: Like the new car you got when you turned eighteen, Fred?
FRED: I worked hard for that car.
DEBBIE: Worked hard to be Mom's favorite so she'd get it for you, maybe. Honestly, Fred, your memory gets so short when it serves your purposes.
LUCY: Since you have such a good memory, Debbie, you must remember all the things that you got to do that Fred and I could never have gotten away with.
DEBBIE: I'm the baby. Nobody ever let me do anything.
LUCY: You call a weekend in New York with your three best friends as a high school graduation gift not doing anything? You know what I got for a graduation present? A trunk to pack for college!
FRED: Forget graduation. What about our proms? I had to be in by one because Mom insisted that I be in church the next morning.
DEBBIE: At least you went to your prom.
LUCY: *(moaning)* Oh, not that again.
DEBBIE: What?
FRED: Debbie, no one kept you from going to your prom. You boycotted it because Mom wouldn't pay for a chauffeured limousine. *(nasal and whiny)* "But, Moooommm, it's only $150. It's not like it's a big deal."
DEBBIE: It was not that much!
LUCY: It's so easy for him to point fingers. Mr. I-Get-More-Christmas-Presents-Than-Anyone-in-the-World.
FRED: Man, have you lost contact with reality!
LUCY: Not at all. Debbie and I would be done unwrapping our couple of tiny, little presents; and we'd look over, and you'd barely have started on your huge pile of lavish gifts.
LUCY: *(standing)* Wait. I have an idea.
FRED: Someone get a news crew.
LUCY: We're not going to resolve this on our own.
FRED: We never do.
LUCY: Let's just ask Mom.
DEBBIE: Great idea.
FRED: You want to have Mom tell you to your face that Lucy's her favorite? You're a masochist, Debbie.

Lucy: Fred, put a lid on it, will you?

Debbie: *(calling)* Mom! *(beat)* MOM!!

Mom: *(offstage)* What is it, dear?

Fred: Oh, of course. "Dear." Debbie's always "dear." And "sweetheart." And "darling."

Debbie: Could you join us out here for a moment?

Mom: *(offstage)* Be right there, sweetheart.

Fred: See? See? Who wants to make a wager on what the answer is going to be? Five bucks on Lucy.

Lucy: Stop it, Fred!

(Mom enters. She wears an apron and wipes her hands on it as she comes in.)

Mom: *(pleasantly)* Okay, Debbie. What's going on out here?

(Fred, Lucy, and Debbie look at each other guiltily. Fred and Lucy gesture for Debbie to ask.)

Debbie: *(very sweet)* Well, Mom, we were just reminiscing about our childhoods, and we can't agree on which one of us was your favorite. Fred said Lucy was. I said Fred was. And silly Lucy thinks I was. Who's right, Mom?

Mom: Oh, that's an easy one.

Fred: It was Lucy, wasn't it?

Mom: No.

Lucy: See? I told you.

Mom: It was none of you.

Fred: What?

Mom: I couldn't play favorites with my children. Each one of you is precious to me. Just as precious as the next one.

Debbie: Really?

Mom: Sure! I loved Fred's hard work and discipline. You put yourself so fully into any project. I loved Debbie's helpfulness. You did those little extra things without being asked. And I loved Lucy's maturity. You impressed me with the wisdom of your decisions from such an early age. I loved each one of you equally and completely. I still do. Each one of you is special, and that's why I love you all so much.

(Fred, Lucy, and Debbie exchange guilty looks again.)

Debbie: I told you so. But you two never listen to me.

Lucy: Give it a rest, Debbie.

Mom: You three must be hungry. How does apple pie, fresh out of the oven, sound?

Fred: Sounds great!

(Fred, Lucy, and Debbie jump up and hurry out to the kitchen. Mom follows them, shaking her head. She stops, looks heavenward and shrugs. She exits.)

Judas Iscariot

Characters: Jesus, Judas
Costumes: Robes of the period

(JESUS sits center stage. JUDAS approaches him slowly, thoughtfully. JESUS looks up at him, studies him a moment, then looks away again.)

JESUS: "I tell you the truth, one of you will betray me."[6]

JUDAS: Oh, come on, Jesus. You've been working too hard for too long. The strain is beginning to show. Why would one of us want to betray you?

JESUS: You tell me, Judas.

JUDAS: There's no reason on earth that I can think of. We're your friends. Don't forget that. I mean, look at us. We gave up everything to follow you, to work with you. After all we've been through, you think one of us would betray you?

JESUS: I know one of you will.

JUDAS: Someone's been lying to you. Planting doubts in your mind. Come on, Jesus. We all go way back — to the beginning. If you can't trust us, who can you trust? The Pharisees?

(JUDAS laughs at his own joke. JESUS does not laugh, keeping a steady gaze on Judas. JUDAS shifts uneasily under his gaze.)

JUDAS *(CONT)*: Man, I really think you're overreacting here. We're out in the streets every day making sure people know about you, about your work. And the people tell us how much they love you, how much they look forward to hearing you preach. Some are even talking about you running for public office. Personally, I think you're more effective working outside the system, but . . .

JESUS: Could it be you, Judas?

JUDAS: What?!?

JESUS: Will you be the one to betray me?

JUDAS: *(shocked whisper)* How can you say that to me? *(getting louder)* How can you even think that? I've been your friend, your ally, your servant. I've risked my neck for you, and yet you can sit there and ask me . . . *(barely contained)* I have never let you down. I've taken care of the treasury, looked after the others, looked after you. How can you insult me like this? Does our friendship mean so little? Do I mean so little?

JESUS: "Woe to that man who betrays the Son of Man! It would be better for him if he had not been born."[7]

(JUDAS moves in an explosion of rage and grabs Jesus. JESUS remains passive. JUDAS raises his hand as though to strike Jesus then freezes as he realizes what he is doing. JUDAS slowly lowers his hand and releases Jesus. JUDAS looks at Jesus for a mournful moment.)

JUDAS: *(softly)* It's not me, Rabbi! It's not me!

JESUS: Yes, it is you.

(JESUS reaches out and embraces the stunned Judas. JUDAS sinks to his knees before him. JESUS places his hands on Judas's head in benediction.)

---

[6]Matthew 26:21

[7]Matthew 26:24

Litany for a Crippled Church

Characters: Leader, People
Costumes: Contemporary

(The LEADER stands to one side and the People—either a chorus or a single individual—stand to the other. Both face forward in an attitude of prayer.)

LEADER: "Go and make disciples of all nations, baptizing them in the name of the Father and of the Son and of the Holy Spirit, and teaching them to obey everything I have commanded you."[8]

(The PEOPLE look over at the Leader in surprise.)

PEOPLE: Excuse me?

LEADER: I said, "Go and make disciples of all nations, baptizing them in the name of the Father and of the Son and of the Holy Spirit, and teaching them to obey everything I have commanded you."

PEOPLE: Whoa. That's what we thought you said. No can do.

LEADER: Excuse me?

PEOPLE: We don't have time for that sort of extra work. We're busy people. We've got things to do, places to be. Plans. Appointments. Double shifts.

LEADER: Aren't you disciples of the church?

PEOPLE: Sure, sure, but that's not the only thing in our lives. We have other stuff. Important stuff.

LEADER: All your time is taken up?

PEOPLE: Just about. There is Tuesday night—but there's this movie we've been wanting to see, and it's on cable, and the VCR's in the shop . . .

LEADER: What about Sunday afternoon?

PEOPLE: Get serious. It's football season.

LEADER: How is the church supposed to go and make disciples?

PEOPLE: C'mon, what do we have pastors for? They get up and do their hour on Sunday—what do they do with the rest of their week?

LEADER: The verse doesn't say, "Just you pastors, go out and make disciples."

PEOPLE: Yeah, well, the wording's pretty vague, you gotta admit.

LEADER: Perhaps you'd prefer different wording.

PEOPLE: That depends.

LEADER: How's this sound? "When and if your schedule permits, please try and take a moment to mention to one person you know that they might want to consider going to church. Tell them you might see them there, unless something comes up, and the pastor will call them later. And if you can't manage to work this in, perhaps you could pass the assignment along to someone else."

PEOPLE: Sounds good to us!

LEADER: I thought you'd like it.

PEOPLE: Well, now that that's taken care of, we're outta here. Bowling league tonight.

LEADER: May Jesus be praised.

PEOPLE: Sure, sure. Whoever he is.

---

[8]Matthew 28:19-20

Rocking the Boat

Characters: Dave, Bill, Steve
Costumes: Robes of the period

(DAVE and BILL stumble onto a rocky beach. They are wet and cold, and they hang onto each other for support. After a few steps, they stumble and collapse to the ground. STEVE stumbles in a few paces behind them. He, too, collapses.)

STEVE: I . . . I can't believe we made it.

DAVE: A dozen times I thought, "We're goners! We're sleeping with the fish tonight."

BILL: I hate that sea. You take your life in your hands every time you push your boat out there.

STEVE: *(clutching his stomach)* I won't be able to eat for a year.

DAVE: I hear you! Last night's fish fry isn't sitting too well.

BILL: We're lucky to be alive.

DAVE: I don't think we would be if he hadn't been with us.

BILL: And he slept through most of it! Slept! Thomas said he heard him snoring! Twelve-foot waves knocking the boat around like a toy, and he's sacked out. Waves crashing across the deck, tossing us around like so many pebbles, and he's snoozing like a baby in a cradle.

STEVE: I've heard of heavy sleepers, but this guy must go catatonic.

DAVE: I finally go over to him and say, "Wake up! We're all going to die!" He turns over and keeps snoring. Everybody's panicking, so I shake him. And shake him and shake him—he's like a bear in hibernation. Finally, he wakes up.

BILL: I saw his face. It was as if he knew exactly what had been happening the whole time he was asleep, and he couldn't understand our panic.

STEVE: And he said, "Quiet. Be still." Then the wind died down and the water went calm . . .
(STEVE shakes his head in awe. All three are quiet for a moment.)

BILL: I'm surprised he didn't just lie back down and go to sleep again.

DAVE: No, it was obviously important to him that he speak to us. I can still hear his words. And see that expression on his face! So filled with sadness, and pain—and frustration.

BILL: I'd gladly trade the pain on his face for the pain in my stomach.

STEVE: Oh, stop complaining. At least you're alive. I'll bet this blasted sea holds the bodies of a few thousand who weren't as lucky.

DAVE: *(thoughtfully)* Was he trying to show us that we could have calmed the water ourselves?

BILL: The storm has rocked your brain, my friend.

DAVE: Maybe. But I think there was a reason we experienced this.

STEVE: I've been thinking the same thing.

BILL: Your common sense washed overboard. You're nuts, both of you.

DAVE: He was teaching us a lesson in faith.

STEVE: Or the lack of it.

BILL: Are you suggesting that with a few well-chosen words, we could have stopped the storm?

DAVE: I know it sounds a little far-fetched.

(BILL rolls his eyes and clutches his head in frustration.)

STEVE: We're not talking magic words here. We're talking about belief—an attitude, a conviction.

DAVE: But not faith in ourselves, faith in him — faith in Jesus. Perhaps he was trying to teach us that it's our faith that will save us. That the waves that rocked the boat are like the world that we encounter every day.

BILL: What's with the philosophy lesson? I'll tell you why the boat rocked! Waves! Big ones! Huge, twelve-foot, extremely wet ones.

STEVE: Until he spoke. Then there was peace.

DAVE: Just when it seemed we could hold on no longer, when we thought we were about to break up on the rocks — calm. Serenity in the middle of the storm. And the strength to sail again. *(beat)* It's a lesson I'll take to heart.

BILL: Take it wherever you like. Just take it downwind. You're starting to smell like overripe seaweed.

STEVE: You don't exactly smell like gardenias, my friend.

BILL: That's why I'm going home to bathe. Is that a custom you're familiar with? I've been meaning to suggest it to you.

(BILL stomps off. STEVE hurries after him.)

STEVE: I've been meaning to suggest that you take a look in the mirror once in a while. But we'll have to find an unbreakable one, I suppose . . .

DAVE: *(firmly)* Quiet. Be still.

(Without acknowledging him, BILL and STEVE continue to argue. They exit. DAVE sighs.)

DAVE *(CONT)*: Hmmm. This may take some practice. Maybe there's a piece missing . . . something I don't understand . . . yet.

(DAVE hurries out after them.)

What About All These Leftovers?

Characters: Narrator, Sam, Eli
Costumes: Robes of the period

(An open field. There are several bushel baskets on the ground. ELI stands over the baskets, writing on a clipboard.)

NARRATOR: "Taking the five loaves and the two fish and looking up to heaven, he gave thanks and broke them. Then he gave them to the disciples to set before the people. They all ate and were satisfied, and the disciples picked up twelve basketfuls of broken pieces that were left over."[9]

(SAM enters, carrying another basket. This basket has a towel draped over the top.)

SAM: Hey, Eli. Got another basket of fish for you.

ELI: Bring it on over, and I'll add it to the official count.

(SAM walks over to Eli. ELI peeks under the towel and turns away in repulsion.)

ELI *(CONT)*: Whew! That's fish all right. Put it over there. Downwind. *(as SAM does so)* Adding these baskets to the ones that were gathered over on the east side of the hill brings us to a dozen baskets.

SAM: Holy halibut! Twelve basketfuls? What are we gonna do with all this fish?

ELI: That's the Final Jeopardy question for today. Jesus didn't leave any instructions, and he went off into the hills for a little R & R.

SAM: Did he head up to Camp David?

ELI: *(a sharp look)* No, Sam, I think they just headed up into the wilds. The whole lot of them. They do it often, or so I hear. I can understand wanting to get away from it all. I'd like to get away from all this fish. I don't know where we're going to put it.

SAM: This was my first miracle, you know. I was really impressed. I mean, Jesus takes those five little loaves and two tiny fish from that little boy and — *voilà*! Everybody gets fed and then some!

ELI: *(nodding)* I was watching him fillet the fish, and I thought, "No, no, cut it into smaller pieces. You won't feed three people cutting hunks like that." And then, before I knew it, we were up to our ears in leftovers.

SAM: Just amazing. I'm so glad I got to see it.

ELI: I only wish Jesus had shown a little restraint. I mean, couldn't he have executed a miracle that provided just enough food for everyone, instead of coming up with one that left us with all this stinking fish?

SAM: Eli! Listen to yourself. A miracle shouldn't be questioned. It should be praised. Besides, there's nothing wrong with leftovers. This is certainly better than not having enough food.

ELI: But what am I supposed to do with twelve bushels of rotting scrod?

SAM: Let's give it away. There are always hungry people around. Let's feed them.

ELI: Look around, Sam. How many hungry people do you see? We're out in the middle of nowhere, and everyone has gone back to town. Who's going to get these twelve bushels back to town?

SAM: Well . . . I could take one. Maybe two. We can make two trips. You and I. And on the second trip, we'll bring reinforcements. Whoever helps us carry the fish gets first dibs when we get back to town.

---

[9]Luke 9:16-17

ELI: *(shaking his head)* I don't know.

SAM: Eli, why are you being such a grouch? Rejoice in this miraculous day!

ELI: It's stuck in my craw, Sam.

SAM: A fishbone, Eli?

ELI: No, this whole leftover thing. Jesus wouldn't do this without a reason. I feel as though he's telling me something, and I'm not deciphering the message correctly.

SAM: You mean it's a miracle *and* a sign? Wow! What does it mean?

ELI: That's what I'm trying to figure out, Sam.

(SAM and ELI assume thoughtful positions, Sam's more exaggerated than Eli's. After a moment:)

SAM: I got it! Leftovers — left over!

ELI: Excuse me?

SAM: Jesus is telling us that there will be twelve left over. And they will feed us.

ELI: Twelve of what left over from what?

SAM: Ummmm . . . I'm still working on that part.

ELI: The only twelve I can think of is the twelve disciples. And what would they be left over from? The way those twelve eat, I doubt leftovers are ever a problem. I'll bet this isn't the first time Jesus has had to perform this miracle.

SAM: Still, I think this is a message about the disciples.

ELI: Well, if it is, I hope the disciples think ahead, because Jesus sure doesn't. How could he leave without telling me what to do with this fish? Doesn't he know that you have to have a plan?

SAM: I have one. Let's fry the leftover fish. I love the smell of frying fish, don't you?

ELI: Don't be ridiculous. It's Friday. No one eats fish on Fridays.

SAM: Who knows? This could be the start of something big.

The One-way Pray-er

Characters: Pray-er, Pray-er's Voice, Lord
Costumes: Contemporary

(THE PRAY-ER sits on a church pew. Throughout the following scene, the Pray-er is silent and simply gestures to accompany the offstage VOICE. The LORD also remains offstage throughout.)

VOICE: Dear Lord, I just want to praise your name today. You have been so good to me, Lord. I never dared dream that I would one day have this fabulous, powerful job and be making such great money. You've truly blessed me. And I praise you for it.

And who could have imagined that one day I would live in a beautiful, five-bedroom, four-bathroom house with three fireplaces, an in-ground swimming pool, and a corner lot? Not to mention the antique furniture and the art collection. I praise you for all this, Lord.

I praise you, too, Lord, for the awesome season tickets. Fifth row, center court! And that stock split last week — a 20 percent gain in three business days! Bless you, Lord, for blessing me! And I praise you for any of the other good stuff that you're doing for me that I'm not thinking about right now. Amen.

(The PRAY-ER stands and starts to exit.)

LORD: Just a minute, there.

VOICE: Huh? Who's there?

LORD: Who have you been praying to?

VOICE: The Lord.

LORD: So who do you think I am, since I am the I AM?

VOICE: Oh, right. This is somebody's idea of a trick. Who put you up to this?

LORD: Who do you know that can read minds?

VOICE: Oh. Oh. *(as it sinks in)* But . . . why would you want to talk to me?

LORD: You seem like a pretty good kid. I thought it was worth a shot. You seem to like me.

VOICE: Oh, I do, Lord. I love you. I praise your name every chance I get.

LORD: So I've noticed. That's what I want to talk to you about. It's about time you tried a different form of praise — it's called giving.

VOICE: What?

LORD: I didn't think it would ring a bell. Giving. Offering. Donating. You always pray about the things you get, and you never pray about the things you could give. You're like a child on my Son's birthday, all wrapped up in the presents you're receiving, and not thinking at all about the presents you're giving.

VOICE: But . . .

LORD: There's no room for excuses here. I've been patient and generous with you, and it's time you gave some of it back. Give through your witness, through your living, and through your wallet.

VOICE: What was that last one?

LORD: You heard me. If you believe so fervently that I've given all these things to you, you won't mind if I take a bit of it back, will you?

VOICE: Maybe there's something else you'd rather have . . .

LORD: There are lots of other things I want from you, but they won't take the place of supporting the work of my kingdom on earth with your offering. Isn't your stewardship committee starting the annual pledge drive next week?

Voice: I think I heard something about that, yes.

Lord: And how great an increase will you be making in your pledge?

Voice: An increase? You want me to give more than I did last year?

Lord: Do you have more than you had last year? Remember, I already know the answer.

Voice: But Lord, I thought you gave me these things because I was a good person.

Lord: And I thought a good person could be trusted to have priorities. To recognize the true value of time, talent, and treasures. Are you worthy of my trust?

Voice: You bet, Lord. I just was wondering if there was some other way . . .

Lord: Are you worthy of my trust? Or will you disappoint me?

Voice: How does a five percent increase sound, Lord? And I've been thinking about teaching vacation Bible school this year. And pitching in on the project to feed the homeless . . .

Lord: Now that's the kind of praise I like to hear.

The Parable of the Found Daughter

Characters: Daughter, Papa
Costumes: Contemporary

(DAUGHTER is working in the kitchen of her home. From the way she's banging pots and pans around, you can tell she's not very happy.)

DAUGHTER: "Yes, Papa, I'll wash the dishes." "Yes, Papa, I'll fix your favorite meal." "Would you like a pillow, Papa?" "May I fix you a cup of tea?" OHHHH! I can't stand it! *(flinging down her dish towel)* I have had it—for once and for all. Had it. I give twenty-one years of my life to that man, devote my every waking hour to him, and what happens? He gets one glimpse of his lost son staggering down the road, and he goes bonkers. Absolutely loses his mind. You'd think this was the headquarters of the United Way—handing out clothes, money, food. And not just any food. Prime rib! I wanted prime rib on my birthday and didn't get it, but the darling boy shows his scruffy face and—"Would you like a baked potato with that? Sour cream or butter?"

PAPA: *(offstage)* Sweetheart, where are you? In the kitchen?

DAUGHTER: Why should I be anywhere else?

(PAPA enters. He is beaming with joy.)

PAPA: There you are. *(seeing her expression)* Hey. Don't frown like that. You'll get wrinkles.

DAUGHTER: Like you care.

PAPA: Aw, sweetheart . . .

DAUGHTER: Don't you call me "sweetheart." Don't call me "honey." Don't call me anything. There's only one kid around here who matters to you, and it's not me.

PAPA: That's not true, and you know it.

DAUGHTER: Then what's all this red-carpet nonsense for that rotten brother of mine? He treats you like dirt, disappears; and the minute he comes home, you open your heart, home, and wallet to him. What did he do that's so special?

PAPA: He came home!

DAUGHTER: What about me, Papa? I've been here all along. I've stayed with you and worked my fingers to the bone. I did your errands, looked after your business, nursed you when you were sick . . . What do I get in return? Pot roast, if I'm lucky.

PAPA: This is different.

DAUGHTER: *(sarcastic)* No need to point that out. I noticed all by myself.

PAPA: I mean, your brother has been gone. It's as though he'd been dead—we never knew where he was, what he was doing, if he was okay. Now, it's as though he's been resurrected! The death that has pervaded my life these past years has been erased. I am filled with the joy of rebirth and new life!

DAUGHTER: Big whoop. He's back. He probably came back to try and rip you off all over again. He probably forgot that he already cashed out his trust fund. He's been running all over creation, drinking and partying and carrying on—I'm sure that clouds the memory. Or is it your memory that's clouded, Dad? Have you forgotten how he left here without a look back? How he's dragged your name through the mud in every dive he's visited? Am I the only one who cares about any of this? Maybe I'm the fool here. Maybe I should follow my brother's lead and run off like some reprobate. It obviously gets your attention.

PAPA: You've always had my attention. You've always been with me, a good and faithful daughter. Everything I have is yours — my heart and my goods. But your brother has been gone such a long time, and now he's come back. We're complete again. Let's celebrate that good fortune. Let's celebrate his decision to return to us and to life.

DAUGHTER: Excuse me if I don't wave a flag. I've devoted myself to serving you, and he's devoted himself to embarrassing you. What does that get us? Equal treatment. There's no justice in that. Why have I been working so hard all these years?

PAPA: Because you're a good girl.

DAUGHTER: Not anymore. I've seen what the bad kids get, and it's a much better deal. From here on in, consider me bad.

(DAUGHTER storms out. PAPA calls after her.)

PAPA: Not bad, my child. Found. Found and forgiven. And free.

No Thanks

Characters: Narrator, Leper 1, Leper 2, Leper 3, Leper 4, Lepers 5-10 (non-speaking)
Costumes: Robes of the period

(The NARRATOR strides to center stage and strikes a pose. The LEPERS follow closely behind and gather like children around a storyteller. The NARRATOR makes sure he has their full attention before beginning.)

NARRATOR: "On the way to Jerusalem Jesus was going through the region between Samaria and Galilee. As he entered a village, ten lepers approached him. Keeping their distance . . ."

(The LEPERS scamper away from the Narrator and arrange themselves in a group, all looking across the stage to an unseen Jesus.)

NARRATOR *(CONT)*: ". . . they called out, saying . . ."

LEPER 2: *(calling)* Jesus!

LEPER 3: Master!

LEPER 4: *(falling to knees)* Have mercy on us!

NARRATOR: "When he saw them, he said to them, 'Go, show yourselves to the priests.' "

(The LEPERS begin to move across stage.)

NARRATOR *(CONT)*: "And as they went, they were made clean."[10]

(The LEPERS continue their trek. The NARRATOR waves to get their attention. LEPER 1 looks over and stops. The other LEPERS stop, looking uncertainly at LEPER 1 and at each other. The NARRATOR makes an "okay" gesture to Leper 1. LEPER 1 scratches his head thoughtfully, trying to understand the gesture. In raising his arm, he notices his skin. It's clear. He examines his arm closely, then holds it up in triumph.)

LEPER 1: Hallelujah!

(The other LEPERS start and huddle together apprehensively. LEPER 1 thrusts his clean arms in front of them. The other LEPERS look in disbelief and awe. LEPER 1 takes their arms in turn to show them that they are also healed. The LEPERS embrace and dance in joy.)

LEPER 1: We are healed!

LEPER 2: Cleansed and saved!

LEPER 3: I can't believe it. After all this time.

LEPER 4: No more hiding in alleys and dark corners.

LEPER 2: No more being pushed aside to make way for the "healthy" folks.

LEPER 1: It's a miracle.

LEPER 3: For once we were in the right place at the right time.

LEPER 2: A first for all of us, I would say.

LEPER 1: We have to go back. Come on.

LEPER 4: Go back to what? The place where we did all our suffering? The site of our humiliation? No. Let's go on and make a new start.

(LEPERS 5-10 dash offstage. LEPER 4 starts away, but LEPER 1 catches his arm. LEPERS 2 and 3 linger to listen.)

LEPER 1: No, no. We have to go back to see him.

LEPER 2: Why?

LEPER 1: Why? To thank him, of course.

LEPER 4: Forget it.

---

[10]Preceding Scripture quotes are from Luke 17:11-14, NRSVB.

Leper 1: No. I'll never forget it. Or him.

Leper 4: What I mean is I'm sure he knows we're grateful. What's the point in going all the way back to tell him so?

Leper 3: Besides, I'm sure he's busy. There are lots of other people to cure.

Leper 2: Haven't we already taken enough of his time?

Leper 1: Wait. This man answers our pleas for mercy. He takes away the very affliction that has made us outcasts. And you won't go back to thank him?

Leper 4: We have things to do. *(Lepers 2 and 3 murmur in agreement.)* We have whole lives to catch up on.

Leper 3: We've been cheated of so many experiences. We can't waste any more time, or we'll never get to everything.

Leper 3: Time is precious. Talk is cheap. We'll send him a postcard from the first place we stop. How's that sound?

Leper 1: *(quietly)* But he healed us.

Leper 4: That was very charitable of him, and I'm sure he enjoyed it as much as we did. But do you think he's obsessed with it? No. He's moved on to the next task, and so should we. *(to Lepers 2 and 3)* Paaaarty! *(They exchange handshakes.)*

Leper 1: So we're no different than all the people who scorned us for the past twenty years; no different than the thousands who heard our cries and looked the other way because they had their own lives, their own problems, their own parties to worry about. They couldn't be bothered. Is this what our lives have come to?

Leper 4: Lighten up, would you? Why is this thank-you such a big deal? What will it change?

Leper 1: Why won't you say it?

Leper 4: Because I don't owe anyone anything.

Leper 1: Not even him? Didn't you cry to him for mercy?

Leper 4: A lifetime ago. Before I was a real person.

Leper 2: Back when we were untouchables.

Leper 1: And yet, he touched you.

Leper 3: You make him sound like God.

Leper 1: Perhaps he is.

Leper 4: Don't talk blasphemy.

Leper 1: Has any common person tried to touch our lives? Haven't the religious officials told us we must have done unspeakable acts against God to be afflicted as we were? Who would have mercy on us—who of this world?

(Pause.)

Leper 4: I'm sorry. I am not going to let you spoil this day with these guilt trips. Life is too short. I have some major celebrating to do. First round's on me for anyone who's interested.

(Lepers 2, 3, and 4 begin to exit. Leper 1 watches them.)

Leper 1: Just a simple thank-you. Is that too much to ask when someone has changed—has saved—your life? Two simple words. *(sighs)* Guess I'll be different one more time.

(Leper 1 turns and begins to exit the opposite way. The Narrator watches him with a proud smile. Leper 1 turns back uncertainly; the Narrator makes the "okay" gesture. Leper 1 smiles and returns it as he exits.)

Who Is the Greatest?

Characters: Narrator, Jesus, Disciples 1-3
Costumes: Robes of the period

(The three DISCIPLES sit at various points on the stage. JESUS moves among them. The NARRATOR stands to the side. Only JESUS looks at anyone else.)

NARRATOR: "After taking the cup, he gave thanks and said, . . ."

JESUS: "Take this and divide it among you. For I tell you I will not drink again of the fruit of the vine until the kingdom of God comes."

NARRATOR: "And he took bread, gave thanks and broke it, and gave it to them, saying, . . ."

JESUS: "This is my body given for you; do this in remembrance of me."

NARRATOR: "In the same way, after the supper he took the cup, saying, . . ."

JESUS: "This cup is the new covenant in my blood, which is poured out for you."[11]

NARRATOR: And the disciples began to argue about which of them was considered to be greatest.

DISCIPLE 1: Get real. Who are you guys trying to kid anyway? I've earned the right to be called the greatest. Remember that crowd of people in Jericho a couple of years ago? When Jesus wasn't available to speak, who did they ask for instead? Huh? They asked for me. Got that? Me.

DISCIPLE 2: Yeah, I put a lot of stock in what a mob says in the heat of the moment. Let's talk long-term here, shall we? I have been the most consistent member of Jesus' cabinet — in every way. Steady, loyal, always by his side. When he needed someone to talk to, who did he come see? Not the Great Public Speaker over there *(gesturing to Disciple 1)*. He came to me. Me.

DISCIPLE 3: Well, now. I sure don't want to burst y'all's bubble, but try this on for size. Who was voted most likely to succeed by his high school class? Who did the *Jerusalem Chronicle* tag as the up-and-coming religious figure for the next decade? And who even looks more like Jesus that anyone else here? It's me. Me.

JESUS: "The kings of the Gentiles lord it over them; and those who exercise authority over them call themselves Benefactors. But you are not to be like that. Instead, the greatest among you should be like the youngest, and the one who rules like the one who serves."

DISCIPLE 3: Now hang on there a minute, Jesus. Are you saying that the greatest will not necessarily have the best résumé, the most press clippings, and the highest position?

JESUS: "Who is greater, the one who is at the table or the one who serves?"

DISCIPLE 1: Is this a trick question?

JESUS: Would you not say that it is the one at the table?

DISCIPLE 2: Absolutely. Without a doubt.

JESUS: "But I am among you as one who serves. You are those who have stood by me in my trials."[12]

(DISCIPLES 1, 2, and 3 take a deep breath as though they are about to respond, but they stop, baffled. Slowly, they lower their heads.)

---

[11]Preceding Scripture quotes are from Luke 22:17-20.

[12]Preceding Scripture quotes are from Luke 22:25-28.

NARRATOR: And it was then that they began to understand that the first shall be the last, the greatest in heaven will be those who have humbled themselves before the Lord here on earth. They understood for the first time exactly what following Jesus would mean: present suffering for future rewards. For a few moments, the room was very, very quiet.

A Cross to Bear

Characters: Simon, Martha
Costumes: Robes of the period

(MARTHA is setting the table for supper. SIMON enters, holding his back and hobbling in pain.)
SIMON: Martha! Help me, please!
(MARTHA rushes over and helps him into a chair.)
MARTHA: Simon! What have you done? Is it your back? *(SIMON nods.)* What will your doctor say? What did you do this time? Try to pick up a bushel of beans without bending from the knees?
SIMON: I wasn't carrying beans, Martha. I was carrying a cross.
MARTHA: A what?
(MARTHA puts her hand on his forehead. SIMON pushes it away.)
SIMON: A cross, Martha. I carried a man's cross.
MARTHA: Simon, how many times do I have to tell you, you don't have to volunteer for everything?
SIMON: I didn't volunteer. I was volunteered. They pulled me from the side of the street. I was just standing there . . . watching. The streets were lined for blocks, and I wanted to get a look at what the fuss was all about. I squeezed my way up to the curb and saw him coming.
MARTHA: You threw your back out for some common criminal?
SIMON: This man was far from common, Martha. And while the Romans called him a criminal, I think he was far from that also. There were two men with him, both with crosses too. Now those two were criminals, but not this man. Anyway, as he got closer I could tell that the weight of the cross was overwhelming him. It was too much for him to bear. He stumbled, got up, stumbled again. And then, right in front of me, he practically collapsed.
MARTHA: And you had to leap forward and save the day.
SIMON: Not at all. I was just standing there, staring. One of the Romans grabbed me and said, "Bear the cross, Jew!" I tried to protest, tried to explain about my bad back, but the soldier just laughed. He grabbed me by the collar and yanked me out into the street. Before I could straighten up, he'd put the cross on my back.
MARTHA: I hate it when you go into the city. Maybe we should move. I'm hardpressed to think of one time that you've gone into that city and nothing bad has happened.
SIMON: Martha, you're being melodramatic. You know, it wasn't really that bad. And when the man looked at me, I saw the strangest expression on his face. It was . . . compassion.
MARTHA: Compassion? A condemned criminal took the time to feel compassion for you, Simon? You're hallucinating.
SIMON: It sounds that way, I know. But it's true. I felt as if he were offering me support for the weight of the cross.
MARTHA: It obviously wasn't enough support.
SIMON: My back will heal, Martha.
MARTHA: Did you carry the cross all the way to the top of the hill?
SIMON: Yes. And when they took the cross from my back, I stayed and watched them prepare him for death. He never protested, never cried out for mercy.
MARTHA: Who was this man? Did you get a name?

Simon: It was Jesus. You know, the one everyone's been talking about.

Martha: The healer?

Simon: Healer. Teacher. Worker of miracles. And perhaps, the Son of God.

Martha: *(feeling his forehead again)* Simon! You are hallucinating. The Son of God? Please. Would he have allowed himself to be treated like a common criminal if he were the Messiah? That's absurd.

Simon: I know it's contrary to all that the rabbis teach about the Messiah, but after what I've seen today, I'm beginning to think it's the truth.

Martha: How can it be? The Messiah would have led us in victorious revolution against our oppressors. He would have saved himself from such a mockery of a death.

Simon: I know, I know. I've been going over these arguments in my head each aching step of the journey home. It doesn't make sense, but it does make sense. It shouldn't have been, but it seems to have been.

Martha: Oh, Simon. Stop. You're getting involved. Forget about it. It's not your cross to bear any longer.

Simon: Yes, it is my cross to bear. I must know more. What if we killed the Messiah that the prophets have told us about for so long?

Martha: What's done is done. He's gone.

Simon: Yes, but his disciples are still here. Some were at the execution. Tomorrow I'm going to search for them. Maybe they can tell me more.

Martha: Oh, Simon, why? Why must you persist?

Simon: I still feel the weight of that cross, Martha. I think I'm going to feel it for a very long time.

Getting Your Hopes Raised

Characters: Henry, Edith
Costumes: Contemporary

(HENRY sits reading the newspaper. EDITH enters, wringing her hands. She hovers briefly then turns on the television. She looks at the screen for a moment then begins pacing, still wringing her hands. HENRY peers over the top of his newspaper.)

HENRY: Why turn on the TV if you aren't going to sit down and watch it? *(EDITH continues pacing.)* What's with the pacing, Edith? You been drinking too much coffee or something?

EDITH: I can't help it, Henry.

HENRY: Of course you can help it. Just sit down. You're wearing a path in the carpet.

EDITH: Henry, I'm too excited to sit down. Today is the day. Today is the final drawing in the Home-Viewer Puzzle Sweepstakes. I know I got the right answer. I know I won. I'm so excited I can barely stand it!

HENRY: *(lowering paper)* What makes you think you got the right answer?

EDITH: It's obvious. *(He makes a face.)* Let me show you, okay?

HENRY: Fine. Make a believer out of me.

EDITH: The answer is two words. The first word has four letters. The second has seven. Are you with me so far?

HENRY: *(bored)* Every step of the way.

EDITH: And the clue is, "It sometimes gets bent out of shape."

HENRY: *(thinks a moment, then)* Ahhh. I got it. "Your husband."

EDITH: Ha ha. Are you interested in this, or not? There's another clue. "The last letter in the first word and the third letter in the second word are an 'e'." *(pause)* Don't you see it, Henry?

HENRY: Ahhh . . .

EDITH: "Pipe cleaner"! It sometimes gets bent out of shape. Get it? A pipe cleaner? It's so obvious.

HENRY: I like my answer better.

EDITH: Well, it doesn't fit. And mine does. I mean, what else can it be?

HENRY: I don't know, Edith, but I'm sure there are lots of possible answers.

EDITH: Like what? It can't be twist ties or Play-Doh or even a car fender. It's got to be a pipe cleaner.

HENRY: Okay, Edith. Suppose you do have the right answer, though I doubt you do. Don't they still have to draw your name from all the contestants who got the right answer?

EDITH: Yes. But I'm sure I'm the only one who got the right answer.

HENRY: Come on, Edith! There's probably thousands of people who got the right answer. And you may or may not be one of them. Aren't you getting your hopes up just a tad?

EDITH: I know I'm the winner, Henry. I can feel it. And get a load of what I'll win. A trip for two anywhere in the world, $50,000 in cash, and a complete, mint-condition set of 1952 Topps baseball cards.

HENRY: Edith, calm down. You're getting yourself all worked up for something that's not going to happen. I'm telling you.

EDITH: Thank you so very much for the vote of confidence, dear. I believe in this, Henry. I have a right to hope. You're not going to stop me. Now, if you would please keep your negative opinions to yourself, it's time for the show to start.

(EDITH steps forward and turns up the television.)

ANNOUNCER: *(offstage)* And now, it's time to reveal the lucky winner of our Home-Viewer Puzzle Sweepstakes. The lucky winner will receive a free trip for two to any location in the world, $50,000 in cash, and a complete, mint-condition set of 1952 Topps baseball cards.

HENRY: I tell you, Edith, there's about as much a chance of your winning this as there is . . . for someone to be raised from the dead.

EDITH: Hush!

ANNOUNCER: *(offstage)* Can you believe it? The winner is the only person out of ten million entries to have the right answer.

(EDITH nudges Henry.)

HENRY: Don't get your hopes up. You don't have a ghost of a chance.

ANNOUNCER: *(offstage)* The one person who gave us the right answer is Mrs. Edith Gibson of Mason, Michigan. The answer was "pipe cleaner." Congratulations, Edith!

(EDITH cheers in victory. HENRY drops his paper and stares at the TV in disbelief.)

Righteous Dudes

Characters: Judith, Victor, Virginia, Jim, Sam, Peter, John
Costumes: Contemporary

(A meeting room. JUDITH, VICTOR, VIRGINIA, JIM, and SAM sit around a conference table. They are all conservatively, perhaps severely, dressed. Each has a file folder brimming with papers.)

JUDITH: Next order of business. *(sighs)* If we're all ready, it's time to bring in Peter and John. I think you're all well aware that we've had a lot of complaints from people about the activities these two have been involved in. Our purpose tonight as the leaders of this church is to assess the damage they've done and determine how we can go about saving our youth program.

VICTOR: Judith, I understand your concern, but let's not overreact. We owe these guys a fair hearing before we decide there's been any damage done at all.

JUDITH: I wish I could be that optimistic, Victor. Sam, would you bring them in?

(SAM rises and exits into another room.)

VIRGINIA: I think Judith's right. It's already out of control. Our youth group is starting to look like a youth gang.

JUDITH: Thank you, Virginia.

(SAM returns with PETER and JOHN. They are dressed like gang members — lots of leather, some chains, etc. PETER wears a bandana and JOHN sports an earring.)

PETER: Homes, good to see you tonight.

JIM: Homes?

JOHN: Yeah, Jim. Homeboys. *(nodding to the women)* And girls. Friends. Neighbors.

PETER: *(making a solidarity gesture)* Brothers and sisters.

JUDITH: Yes. Well . . . how nice. *(awkward pause)* Peter, John, we've received a number of complaints. We've called you here tonight to discuss and address this urgent matter.

PETER: Complaints about what?

VIRGINIA: You had a drug pusher here last week! Some horrible person that the children referred to as Tony B. went to a youth group meeting. Sat with our children!

JUDITH: Virginia . . .

VIRGINIA: *(collecting herself)* Sorry.

PETER: Tony B. sat in on a meeting. So?

VIRGINIA: So? The creature is a drug pusher, a man who makes his living selling illegal narcotics to boys and girls like the ones in our youth group, and you say, "So?" How dare you!

PETER: Chill. Let's tell the whole story, okay? Tony B. was hanging that night because he came to us for help. We shared with him the Good News that is Jesus Christ, and Tony B. accepted Christ as his savior that very night. If we're getting ragged on for bringing a lost soul to salvation, you'd best remember this: It's by the name of Jesus Christ that Tony B. works with our young people today, spreading the Gospel with them instead of selling drugs to them. The Spirit of the Lord is more alive in Tony B. than it is in a dozen church leaders.

SAM: I beg your pardon.

PETER: Guilty conscience, Sam?

JOHN: You want Jesus to be all neat and pretty, like we were shooting *The Greatest Story Ever Told*. But that's not how it goes down. Jesus looks like anyone who needs him,

homes. Jesus is for all of us, and he's for each of us. Don't sterilize him. Let him live among us.

JIM: But your approach is so . . . We've never done it this way.

JOHN: What way do you do it, Jim?

JIM: We're accustomed to seeing our young people dressed decently, well-groomed, and very well-trained in the Scriptures. But the two of you are turning them into *(gesturing at them)* . . . renegades.

PETER: Just like us, huh, Jim?

JIM: I didn't say that.

PETER: But you can't stop thinking it, can you? Admit it! You're worried your son is going to come home from a youth group meeting one night looking like me. Right? And you want him to look like your idea of the perfect Christian. You want him to look like you. *(stripping off his jacket)* There. That better?

JIM: Now just a moment . . .

JUDITH: Gentlemen, control yourselves.

PETER: Oh, of course. Let's not show anger. Let's not show passion. Let's not show anything at all. Let's sit in the little church with our hands folded in our laps and think about what wonderful lives we lead. That's not what it's all about, folks. That's not what Jesus would be doing if he were walking among us right now. He'd be doing what we're doing — getting out in the streets, meeting the people who need him, helping them, working with them, loving them.

JUDITH: But you were hired to work with our youth, not with street people.

PETER: I was called to bring your youngsters to a closer relationship with the Lord. I can't do that if all we do is sit around the piano and sing camp songs. John and I are teaching by example, showing them how to reach out and live their faith. And they're doing it. And they're good at it, too. Why does that embarrass you? You should be proud.

VIRGINIA: Let me tell you how proud I am when I hear my neighbors talking about the goings on at this church.

JIM: We've already lost a few families because of your antics. Families that were faithful givers.

PETER: Is that how you evaluate your ministry? Gossip and dollars? When you stand on the Rock, you don't worry about what other people say and do. When you serve Jesus as he's called you to serve, your life has purpose and direction. All the pettiness falls away.

VICTOR: Peter's right. We're worried about the wrong things here. If Peter and John were teaching the youth incorrectly, we would have a genuine complaint. But they're teaching the gospel by putting it into action. We should be complimenting them, not chastising. And if the vigor of their faith makes us uncomfortable, maybe we should be chastising ourselves.

VIRGINIA: Whose side are you on, Victor?

JIM: If you two want to minister to junkies and pushers and any other low-life type you fancy, go ahead and do it — but not on my property and not on my budget. This is a church, for heaven's sake!

JOHN: A church, a school, a street corner — it's all the same to Peter. He can bring kids to Christ in a video arcade. Can't you see? He's sincere. He lives his faith. The kids respect that. They relate to it. They come to church because of him, not because of anything you do. Stuffed shirts like you keep them away.

JIM: Hold on a minute . . .

PETER: No, you hold on. The Lord has given us a ministry. We're not in it for riches or glory or comfort. We do it because he called us. We do it because it must be done. We'll keep doing it, but I guess we'll be doing it somewhere else. *(picking up his jacket)* Keep the faith, homes.

(PETER exits. JOHN salutes the church leaders and exits after Peter. There is a moment of silence.)

VIRGINIA: *(brightly)* Well, I guess that's that. What's next?

(VICTOR rises. JUDITH, VIRGINIA, JIM, and SAM look at him in surprise.)

JUDITH: Victor? Is there something wrong?

VICTOR: Yes. No question about it. You think we just solved a problem? Our problems have just begun. *(VICTOR salutes them as John did.)* Keep the faith, homes.

(VICTOR exits.)

Barney's Rubles

Characters: Narrator, Peter, Matthew, Thomas, Mark, Barney
Costumes: Robes of the period

(PETER, MATTHEW, THOMAS, and MARK sit around a large table. They are going through paperwork. They are not happy.)

NARRATOR: "All the believers were one in heart and mind. No one claimed that any of his possessions was his own, but they shared everything they had. With great power the apostles continued to testify to the resurrection of the Lord Jesus, and much grace was with them all. There were no needy persons among them. For from time to time, those who owned lands or houses sold them, brought the money from the sales and put it at the apostles' feet, and it was distributed to anyone as he had need. Joseph, a Levite from Cyprus, whom the apostles called Barnabas, sold a field he owned and brought the money and put it at the apostles' feet."[13]

PETER: Moving on. The treasurer's report. How's it look, Matthew?

MATTHEW: Peter, I hate to be the bearer of less-than-glad tidings, but our Fellowship Fund is beginning to look as dry as the Egyptian desert.

PETER: Meaning?

MATTHEW: We need cash!

THOMAS: Perhaps we're being too enthusiastic in our giving to the poor.

PETER: But that's exactly the way Jesus taught us to give. With joy. With enthusiasm.

MATTHEW: Money in the bank wouldn't hurt either.

MARK: It's true, Peter. If the outgoing is more than the incoming, we'll have to make some changes or the organization will be in big trouble.

MATTHEW: I agree with Mark. Deficit spending is a terrible trap. You dig a hole and never get out. Besides, the people will think we're awfully poor stewards if we start spending money we don't have.

THOMAS: I can just see it. The deficit will grow and grow and grow, and soon we'll be sitting on a deficit of two hundred billion rubles.

PETER: Not in a million years, Thomas.

MATTHEW: Nevertheless, Peter, we have to do something.

MARK: If only Jesus were still here. We could do a series of Friday-night fish fries. Think of what we could net—financially speaking—with him around. He had such a way with fish. And bread, too.

PETER: The Lord will still supply our needs. We must have faith and continue the work. The rest will come.

(BARNEY enters, carrying a large bag of coins.)

BARNEY: Excuse me, brothers. Have I come at a bad time?

MATTHEW: Barnabas! How nice to see you.

BARNEY: Please, call me Barney.

MATTHEW: Come in, Barney. Join us.

PETER: What can we do for you, Barney?

BARNEY: Oh, I don't need anything. But there are so many others who do. And your group is so good about helping. . . . Brothers, I want you to have this.

(BARNEY holds out the bag of coins. MATTHEW takes the bag and reacts with surprise at its

---

[13]Acts 4:32-37

weight. MATTHEW peers into the bag and looks at Barney with even greater surprise.)

MATTHEW: This is full of rubles.

BARNEY: I had this field that I wasn't really doing much with, so I sold it. Land values are way up, and it made sense to sell. I was trying to decide how to invest the money, and I thought, Barney, invest in your fellow human beings. Go see that nice bunch of apostles, and let them do good things for the less fortunate with your bag of rubles.

MARK: We assure you, Barney's rubles will be put to good use.

PETER: May the Lord bless you abundantly because of your gift.

BARNEY: That's the great part. God blessed me before—I got the land. God blessed me again—I got a good price. And God blesses me yet again—by introducing me to you fine folks, so I can participate in your work. In my own small way.

PETER: It's a great way, Barney. *(to the others)* Here we see the Lord in action, brothers. I told you he would provide.

BARNEY: Provided we believe.

PETER: Amen to that!

ALL: Amen!

Falling on Deaf Minds

Characters: Jud, Francis
Costumes: Contemporary

(JUD is watching TV, remote control at the ready. There is a knock on the door. JUD calls without taking his eyes off the set. JUD flips channels with the remote throughout and rarely looks away from the TV.)

JUD: Come on in! Door's open!

(FRANCIS enters and hovers uncertainly near Jud's chair.)

FRANCIS: Hi, Jud.

JUD: Hey, Francis. What's shakin'? Pull up a chair.

FRANCIS: Jud, do you have a few minutes? I really need to talk.

JUD: Are you kidding? My time is your time. My ears are your ears. My chairs are your chairs. My big-screen, stereo, high-resolution TV is your . . .

FRANCIS: Jud! I get the picture.

JUD: Oh. Right. So what's on your mind?

FRANCIS: *(sitting)* I'm really depressed, Jud. I had a physical a couple of weeks ago, and the doctor didn't like what he saw in the blood work. I had to have a whole batch of extra tests done, and the doctor just called. He wants me to come in tomorrow morning so we can talk. Jud, I've got cancer. I know it. My grandfather had it, my uncle Howard died of it last year. I know that's what it is.

JUD: I remember when your uncle died. We'd just been to that great Lions game, and the message was waiting for you when we got home. Remember?

FRANCIS: *(nodding)* It was a very sad day.

JUD: Sad day? Are you kidding? Eddie Murray kicked a fifty-three-yard field goal with three seconds to go. Poetry in motion! Of course, the Lions still lost by forty-three, so I guess it could be considered a sad day.

FRANCIS: Jud, listen to me. What if I have cancer? What about my family? Why is this happening?

JUD: Aw, Francis, take it easy. I bet you're fine. I bet come Super Bowl time you're still with us. And I bet it'll be the Saints and the Bengals in the Bowl.

FRANCIS: How can you say that?

JUD: Because the Broncos have no backfield. It's plain as day.

FRANCIS: Jud! I might be dying! Could we please discuss something other than football?

JUD: Sorry, Francis. You know I've never been much of a baseball fan.

FRANCIS: Jud. I thought you were my friend.

JUD: I am your friend. Who was at your side with the latest edition of *Sporting News* when you were laid up with that sprained ankle?

FRANCIS: You made me reimburse you for the paper and your mileage.

JUD: And I drove a lot of miles to get a copy that was in good shape. Who else would have done that for you?

FRANCIS: It probably would have been cheaper to have had it sent Federal Express from the publisher.

JUD: That's gratitude for you. I missed the opening tip-off of the Slippery Rock-Buffalo State game to do it, and this is the thanks I get.

FRANCIS: Excuse me. I guess it's not very considerate to belittle the thoughtfulness of your actions. I'm sorry, Jud. I'm just so nervous about these test results . . .

JUD: Take it easy, Francis. They've come a long way in treating cancer. I'm sure you'll be fine. And if you're not, I still bet you have more time left than you think.

FRANCIS: *(looks at him in amazement for a moment)* Thanks for the encouragement.

JUD: Sure. Hey, how about those Bears last Monday night? Were they awesome or what?

FRANCIS: *(nodding slowly)* Yeah, they were sure something. Well, I'll let you get back to your game. Thanks for listening to me, Jud.

(FRANCIS starts to exit. JUD, eyes never leaving the TV screen, waves vaguely to him.)

JUD: Hey, Francis. Anytime. I'm here for you. What are friends for? You just call me when you need something, pal. You need to talk, you know who to come to. Make sure the door latches on your way out, okay?

FRANCIS: No problem.

(FRANCIS exits. JUD leans forward in his chair, flipping channels.)

JUD: Man, I cannot believe he would come over during "Wide World of Sports." Good thing the football game hasn't started yet. Some people are so inconsiderate.

The Letter—and Volume—of the Law

Characters: Deborah, Policeman, Narrator
Costumes: Contemporary

(DEBORAH is at the wheel of her car. She is driving and humming "Amazing Grace." After a moment, there is the sound of a siren offstage. DEBORAH checks her rearview mirror.)

DEBORAH: Oh, no! A cop! He can't be after me. What did I do? Nothing. *(She pulls over.)* I don't need this.

(A POLICEMAN enters and walks up to Deborah's window. He smiles politely.)

POLICEMAN: Good morning, ma'am.

DEBORAH: *(brightly)* Good morning to you, officer. Is there a problem?

POLICEMAN: May I see your license and registration, ma'am?

DEBORAH: Certainly! *(digging in her purse)* It's not my tags, is it? I know I just changed those. Do I have a brake light out? It's so hard to know those things unless someone else points them out . . .

POLICEMAN: No, ma'am, your lights seem to be in order.

DEBORAH: *(handing him papers)* License and registration. Then what's the problem, officer?

POLICEMAN: You failed to stop for a red light. You were also speeding.

DEBORAH: What? A red light? I never ran a red light!

POLICEMAN: Unfortunately, you did exactly that, ma'am.

DEBORAH: Where was there a red light?

POLICEMAN: Two blocks back, ma'am. Intersection of Broad and Walnut.

DEBORAH: *(shrill)* I was looking. I was paying attention. There was no light.

POLICEMAN: *(pointing)* Can you see those tree branches above the intersection, ma'am?

(DEBORAH cranes her neck out the window to look.)

DEBORAH: *(impatient)* Yes, I see them. Aren't they lovely.

POLICEMAN: The red light is up there by those branches.

DEBORAH: *(turning back to him)* Up in the branches!! Well, would you please tell me how I'm supposed to see it up there? Am I supposed to be watching the road or gazing at the treetops? Of all the stupid places for a red light . . .

POLICEMAN: It's been there for years, ma'am.

DEBORAH: Well, maybe I've never driven down this street before.

POLICEMAN: Ma'am, I don't make the laws, I just enforce them.

DEBORAH: I couldn't see the light. I swear it.

POLICEMAN: You're welcome to take that up in traffic court, ma'am. You know, it's amazing. I've been on the force for eleven years, and I've yet to have someone admit her guilt—or his, for that matter. There's always a reason, an excuse.

DEBORAH: Well, then, maybe the lights need to be changed.

POLICEMAN: That's a dangerous intersection, ma'am. We need a light there.

DEBORAH: Come on! You have to admit that the light is hard to see.

POLICEMAN: And did that also affect your speed? The speed limit is thirty through here, ma'am.

DEBORAH: And I suppose I was zipping along at some ungodly speed.

POLICEMAN: You were going thirty-one.

DEBORAH: Thirty-one! One mile over the limit, and you're going to give me a ticket?

POLICEMAN: Ma'am, let me ask you a question. What does the term "speed limit" mean?

DEBORAH: It means this is how fast you should go.

POLICEMAN: No, ma'am. It means you must go no faster than this.

DEBORAH: But it was only a mile. One teeny, little mile.

POLICEMAN: Ma'am, as I said, it's my duty to enforce the law. The law says "speed limit, thirty." You were going thirty-one. What if I let you go, and the next person who drives by is going thirty-two? Should I let that driver go without a ticket because he's only going one mile an hour faster than you were? Where would it end, ma'am? The law is the law. It works because it's the same for everyone.

DEBORAH: What about grace? Hmmm? A little flexibility? A little forgiveness? Doesn't that enter in here at all?

POLICEMAN: Sorry, ma'am. Grace is up to the judge; I only enforce the law.

DEBORAH: *(disgusted)* Well, now, I wouldn't want you to do anything that would go against the law.

POLICEMAN: *(handing Deborah her papers)* Your license and registration, ma'am. *(handing her another paper)* And your ticket. Have a nice day and drive safely.

(DEBORAH snatches the ticket from him, and the POLICEMAN exits.)

DEBORAH: There ought to be a law.

NARRATOR: *(offstage)* "The law was added so that the trespass might increase. But where sin increased, grace increased all the more."[14]

---

[14]Romans 5:20

Free Admission

Characters: Pat, Usher
Costumes: Contemporary

(The USHER stands at the sanctuary door, bulletins in hand, perhaps wearing a ribbon or nametag identifying her as an usher. After a moment, PAT enters and pauses apprehensively a small distance from the Usher. The USHER looks at Pat and smiles. Heartened, PAT approaches her tentatively.)

PAT: Excuse me.

USHER: *(holding out a bulletin)* Good morning. Nice to have you with us.

(PAT looks down at the bulletin uncertainly and does not take it.)

PAT: I was wondering . . . Could you help me?

USHER: *(retracting the bulletin; sincere)* Of course. What do you need?

PAT: This is so embarrassing. . . . I can't find the ticket window.

USHER: The ticket window? Ma'am, I'm afraid we don't have one.

PAT: Now I'm confused. Was I supposed to go to Ticketron or something?

USHER: I'm afraid I'm confused too, ma'am. What sort of tickets are you looking for?

PAT: Admission tickets. *(gesturing to sanctuary)* To your church service.

USHER: *(with a relieved smile)* We don't charge admission here. Our doors are open to anyone who would like to join us.

PAT: *(suspicious)* Free admission?

USHER: Absolutely.

PAT: That's strange. *(pause)* You get us on the way out, is that it?

USHER: No, ma'am. There's no charge at all for attending a worship service. Now, we do collect an offering during the service, but it's your personal choice whether or not to give. And you decide how much. Free will is what we call it.

PAT: *(still suspicious)* But my friend at work told me that going to church on Sunday would be more than worth my while. She told me that if I attended, I would gain wonderful advantages, great benefits, and peace of mind.

USHER: That's true. I would say most of us feel exactly that way, and that's why we come back week after week.

PAT: That's very nice, but my experience in the business world has been that you get what you pay for. Anything worth something has a pricetag attached—eventually. I bet this is like one of those cards you get in the mail that tells you you've won a free vacation. I got one of those—a free week at a resort in Tennessee. All I had to do was call the number on the card by a certain time, and the vacation was mine. But when I called the number, I found out the free week was mine as long as I took another week at full price.

USHER: I'm sorry you had a bad experience, but there really are no hidden price tags or gimmicks here. We have always had free admission, and our "customers," if you will, seem consistently pleased with the service.

(PAT looks past the Usher, trying to peek into the sanctuary.)

PAT: So where's the catch?

USHER: There is no catch. Here. Look at one of our bulletins. It describes our service and the many affiliated activities that happen here throughout the week.

(The USHER holds out the bulletin. PAT starts to take it, then stops.)

PAT: Hah! Here we go. How much do you want for the special commemorative program?

Usher: Ma'am, this is just our regular Sunday bulletin. We hand it out every Sunday morning, free of charge.

Pat: How do you people stay in business?

Usher: Actually, we don't think of ourselves as a business.

Pat: But you still have bills to pay. The utility company doesn't provide its services for free, does it?

Usher: No, ma'am, you're right there. We're able to pay our bills and donate money to the community because people donate money to us. People freely give.

Pat: "Free" is a popular word around here.

Usher: In a way, "free" is what we're all about.

Pat: Amazing.

Usher: Amazing grace, to be precise.

Pat: Excuse me?

Usher: Amazing grace is the bottom line in this operation. Jesus Christ has paid for our salvation.

Pat: Tell me more.

Usher: Why don't you come in and have a seat? I think you'll like what you hear.

Pat: Great. *(Pat starts to follow the Usher, but stops.)* Wait. I want to stop at the concession stand first.

Usher: Sorry, ma'am, but we don't have one of those.

Pat: You expect people to get through an entire show without eating?

Usher: Actually, ma'am, we do serve a meal, but that's a whole 'nother story.

Pat: Amazing.

Usher: Yes, ma'am.

(They exit.)

Deathfest V

Characters: Thomas, Dad
Costumes: Contemporary

(DAD is sitting in his easy chair, reading the newspaper. He glances at his watch, then returns to his paper. THOMAS enters, wearing a speed metal T-shirt. THOMAS is playing serious air guitar and singing along as he bounds into the room. He stops and waves at his father.)

THOMAS: Hey, Dad, you're still up!

DAD: I wasn't very sleepy.

THOMAS: It's cool, Dad. I know you were waiting up to make sure I got in under curfew.

DAD: I was a little concerned about this concert you went to tonight.

THOMAS: Deathfest Five! Dad, it was totally excellent!

DAD: I can imagine.

THOMAS: This new group from Canada opened — the Headless Screaming Cobras. They cranked, Dad. Mega-sounds.

DAD: *(a step behind)* Headless Screaming Cobras?

THOMAS: Yeah. They were excellent.

DAD: Thomas, how can a cobra scream if it's headless? Or, for that matter, how can a cobra scream at all?

THOMAS: No more PBS for you, Dadster. You're being way too much of a brain here. It's not real. It's an idea, an image.

DAD: And a charming one at that.

THOMAS: Oh, and then, the Tooth Fairy came out.

DAD: I thought you didn't believe in the tooth fairy anymore.

THOMAS: Not that tooth fairy, Dad, the group. They are the coolest metal dudes ever. Their lead singer screams like he's gonna pop a blood vessel or something. Serious sounds.

DAD: If he's screaming, don't you have trouble understanding what he's saying?

THOMAS: Dad, a concert isn't about listening. It's about hearing. It's about experiencing the total cosmos of the music. You feel it.

DAD: I see.

THOMAS: The best part of all was Billy Bob and the Pinheads. They are definitely my favorite band. I can still feel the bass line right here *(thumping his chest)*. My ears will be ringing until tomorrow.

DAD: I hope that won't interfere with your singing at church.

THOMAS: *(rolling his eyes)* Oh, great. Church. *(He fakes a yawn.)*

DAD: Tomorrow's Sunday, young man, and you are going to get up and go to church, no matter where you've been dancing around tonight. I tell you, son, it worries me a lot that, given a choice between Deathfest Fifteen and anything affiliated with Christianity, you'd go to Deathfest.

THOMAS: Can you blame me? I'm tired of singing "The Old Rugged Cross." It's slow and boring, and it's got a lousy beat. I want music I can feel.

DAD: So you're choosing rock music over God?

THOMAS: I didn't say that. I'll go to church tomorrow. I promise. I'll even go to early service, if that will make you happy.

DAD: This isn't about making me happy. This is about you making choices — of where to spend your time and energy.

THOMAS: Whoa, Dad. Come on. You're making this a big deal.

DAD: It is a big deal. All you can talk about or think about is this . . . music. It disturbs me that it's become a priority in your life.

THOMAS: All right, Dad. I'll go to both services tomorrow. Happy?

DAD: Thomas, if you're going to do me a favor, do me this one. Give up your music for two weeks.

THOMAS: What? Is this a pitch to join the choir?

DAD: No, this is a pitch for silence.

THOMAS: Get real, Dad. I keep the volume down like you asked.

DAD: But is the volume down in your mind? Are you really listening to the messages these bands are putting forth? Do you believe in the world they believe in? Clear your mind, and then take a look at who these people are. Please, son.

THOMAS: I'll think about it, Dad. Good night.

(THOMAS exits. DAD turns to the audience.)

DAD: "Those who live according to the sinful nature have their minds set on what that nature desires; but those who live in accordance with the Spirit have their minds set on what the Spirit desires."[15]

---

[15]Romans 8:5

Separating PB & J

Characters: Sarah, Dad
Costumes: Contemporary

(SARAH, a little girl, is at the kitchen table. She has a loaf of bread, jars of peanut butter and jelly, and utensils. SARAH makes sure everything is laid out properly, then stands on her chair.)
SARAH: *(calling)* Daddy! Daddy!
DAD: *(offstage)* What is it, Sarah?
SARAH: May I have lunch now?
DAD: *(offstage)* What are you hungry for?
SARAH: *(patting the peanut butter jar)* What do we have?
(DAD enters and looks at Sarah and her spread with a smile.)
DAD: I think we have peanut butter and jelly.
SARAH: I think so, too.
DAD: Is that what you want for lunch?
SARAH: Yes, please.
(DAD joins her at the table and begins making a sandwich.)
DAD: All right, one PB & J coming up.
(SARAH watches him intently for a moment.)
SARAH: Dad?
DAD: Yes, honey?
SARAH: How does the jelly get separated from the peanut butter, and the peanut butter from the bread, and the bread from the jelly, once it's in my tummy?
DAD: It doesn't, Sarah. It doesn't need to.
SARAH: But don't the vitamins from the peanut butter go one place, and the vitamins from the jelly go some place else?
DAD: Well, that's later, Sarah. In your tummy it all gets digested together.
SARAH: So when do the peanut butter and the jelly separate?
DAD: They don't, sweetheart. You put the jelly on one slice and the peanut butter on the other . . .
(DAD takes his two prepared slices of bread and places them gently together. SARAH leans over and pounds the slices together with the palm of her hand.)
SARAH: . . . and SMOOSH 'em together!
DAD: Exactly. *(examining the sandwich)* I don't think we'll ever get those apart. They're inseparable now. The peanut butter is in the jelly, and the jelly's in the peanut butter; you can't take them apart again.
SARAH: I feel kinda sad for the peanut butter and the jelly being all mixed up.
DAD: But think of how much better they taste that way, Sarah. Isn't peanut butter and jelly better than peanut butter alone or jelly all by itself?
SARAH: PB & J is the best!
DAD: So be happy that they're great together. Enjoy!
(DAD hands her the sandwich, and SARAH runs happily offstage.)
DAD *(CONT)*: Paul wrote these words in his letter to the Romans: "Who shall separate us from the love of Christ? Shall trouble or hardship or persecution or famine or nakedness or danger or sword? No, in all these things we are more than conquerors through him who loved us. For I am convinced that neither death nor life, neither angels nor demons, neither the present nor the future, nor any powers, neither height nor depth, nor anything else in all creation, will be able to separate us from the love of God that is in Christ Jesus our Lord."[16]

---

[16]Romans 8:35, 37-39

Loves Me, Loves Me Not

Characters: Rachel, Angela
Costumes: Contemporary

(A bare stage. RACHEL stands center with a large flower in her hand. She is intent on pulling off the petals of the flower.)

RACHEL: Loves me, loves me not. Loves me, loves me not.

(ANGELA enters. She walks up to Rachel with a curious frown.)

ANGELA: Rachel, what are you doing?

RACHEL: I'm conducting a scientific investigation into the reality of God's love.

ANGELA: By pulling the petals off a flower?

RACHEL: I figure this way I have at least a 50 percent chance of getting the answer I want. That's the best I can hope for and certainly more than I deserve.

ANGELA: What are you talking about?

RACHEL: As my mother would say, "I've been a bad, bad girl."

ANGELA: What did you do?

RACHEL: Well, it started in art class. I made this totally cool parachute out of fabric we'd been dyeing. I brought it home and thought, "I wonder if this would really work." It was way too small for me, but it was the perfect size for Tickles.

ANGELA: Your cat?

RACHEL: Right. So I put Tickles in the parachute and dropped her out my bedroom window.

ANGELA: Your second-floor bedroom window?

RACHEL: Right. That stuff about landing on all fours no matter what? Don't believe it. Anyway, the parachute was a disaster, but Tickles will be all right. She'll be out of the casts in a month or so.

ANGELA: Casts? Plural?

RACHEL: Yeah, that's the other snag. Mom was pretty cool about taking Tickles to the vet, but when she saw the bill—wow! Uncool.

ANGELA: I bet.

RACHEL: So that's where the "I've been a bad, bad girl" part comes in. So, where was I? *(pulling petals again)* Loves me, loves me not, loves me . . .

ANGELA: Rachel, you can't base God's love on the number of petals on a flower. God's love is infinite, and nothing can take it away from you.

RACHEL: Not even one seriously mangled cat?

ANGELA: I'm sure God isn't happy about what happened to Tickles, but that doesn't mean God's unhappy with you. Nothing can separate you from God's love.

RACHEL: Says who?

ANGELA: My pastor, last Sunday. And it says so in the Bible.

RACHEL: People do some really stupid, ugly things. God still loves them?

ANGELA: God may be unhappy with the actions, but God loves the person.

RACHEL: You mean to tell me that when Billy Duke spit his bubble gum into my hair at the pep rally last week, God didn't hate him for doing that? I sure did.

ANGELA: God hated the action, but loved the person.

RACHEL: And when Molly McBride took five bucks from her mom's purse, bought Ho Hos with it, ate every last one, then threw up on her family's new couch . . .

ANGELA: Hated the action, loved the person. Like your mom after the Tickles incident. I'm sure she was steamed, but she didn't hate you.

RACHEL: I think she was thinking about it.

ANGELA: Rachel, she loves you. God does, too. Nothing you can ever do will make either one stop loving you.

RACHEL: Hey, I'm a lucky girl. Except where cats are concerned.

(ANGELA and RACHEL exit. RACHEL returns to her flower as they go.)

ANGELA: God loves me, God loves me tons, God loves me, God loves me megatons . . .

Paying Taxes

Characters: Clerk, Joseph
Costumes: Contemporary

(An office cubicle at a local IRS office. A CLERK sits at the desk. She hangs up her phone and consults the paperwork on her desk.)

CLERK: *(calling)* Number 313! *(pause)* 313?

(JOSEPH rushes in at breakneck speed.)

JOSEPH: I knew it, I knew it! The minute I get up to get a drink of water, you call my number. I could have sat here all day dying of thirst, and you wouldn't have gotten to me; but the minute I get up . . .

CLERK: Sir.

JOSEPH: Yes?

CLERK: Why don't you have a seat and tell me why you're here today.

JOSEPH: *(sitting in the guest chair)* It's about my taxes.

CLERK: Yes, sir, it generally is. I suppose you think we owe you a refund.

JOSEPH: No, actually, I want to pay my taxes.

CLERK: Oh. One of those. Delinquent tax payments can be made in the cashier's office on the third floor. Be prepared to pay all applicable interest and penalties.

JOSEPH: I don't see why I'd have to pay interest or penalties . . .

CLERK: Why don't you take that up with your congressional representative, sir? I really don't have the time. *(calling)* Number 314!

JOSEPH: But I sent my check in on time. It's just that they sent it back — with a note that said "no further payment necessary."

CLERK: *(stunned)* Excuse me? We gave money back? Money you thought you owed us we returned to you?

JOSEPH: Yes, ma'am, you certainly did.

CLERK: Sir, I've never heard of such a thing. It's impossible.

JOSEPH: Yup, thought the same myself. That's why I'm here. I want to pay my fair share.

CLERK: Sir, if this is your idea of a joke . . .

JOSEPH: Do you see me laughing? I'm looking for some help, ma'am. Are you going to help me, or not?

CLERK: Sir, you can't expect me to believe that the IRS returned your check accidentally and that you're here to insist on paying your tax liability.

JOSEPH: But I am. It's my duty as a Christian.

CLERK: Oh, this gets better by the minute. Your duty as a what?

JOSEPH: As a Christian. And as a citizen. The apostle Paul wrote about this in his letter to the Romans. He said, "Therefore, it is necessary to submit to the authorities, not only because of possible punishment but also because of conscience."[17]

CLERK: If you've got a guilty conscience, mister, go clean it somewhere else. No one comes into my office and insists on paying his taxes.

JOSEPH: Please. I want to do my part. The deficit . . . education funding . . . environmental clean up . . . Someone must want my tax dollars. Won't you take my check?

(JOSEPH holds out a check. With a great sigh, the CLERK takes it.)

CLERK: All right, all right. I'll take it.

---

[17]Romans 13:5

JOSEPH: Thank you. Thank you so much. God bless you.

(JOSEPH hurries out.)

CLERK: Yeah, same to you. *(making sure he's gone)* Wise guy. *(ripping check in half)* Trying to start something here? *(calling)* Number 314! 314, please!

Job Descriptions

Characters: Mrs. Grundy, Apollos, Paul, Cephas, Narrator
Costumes: Contemporary

(A tidy living room, and Mrs. Grundy is doing the tidying. There is a knock at the front door. She crosses to the door and opens it, revealing Apollos, Paul, and Cephas all dressed in matching workers' coveralls.)

Mrs. Grundy: Yes?

Paul: Afternoon, ma'am. We're here about your salvation problem.

Mrs. Grundy: Oh, of course. Come right in. *(as they file by)* Goodness. I'm afraid I wasn't expecting three of you.

Apollos: Oh, yes, ma'am. We always work as a team. Works best that way.

Mrs. Grundy: I think that's just marvelous. It seems as though there's so much competition today, even in churches, with everyone claiming to have saved this many souls or brought that many sheep back into the flock. So unattractive. I think it's lovely that you boys work as a team.

Paul: Thank you, ma'am.

(Apollos, Paul, and Cephas raise their hands in the air, touching extended index fingers.)

Paul, Apollos, and Cephas: One for all, and all for the One!

(They relax.)

Cephas: Now, Mrs. Grundy, could you fill us in on the salvation problem you need fixed?

Mrs. Grundy: It's my son Ahab. It seems like it's been one problem after another since his father died.

Paul: How long ago was that, Mrs. Grundy?

Mrs. Grundy: Goodness, it's been ten years already. Dropped dead in the backyard, hanging clothes on the line.

Paul: So the boy's been without a father figure for some time.

Mrs. Grundy: Poor dear was only eight when we suffered our loss.

Cephas: Do you have any recommendations as to the best approach for us to take to help him accept Jesus as his Lord and Savior?

Mrs. Grundy: I was hoping you could just talk to him. Get to know him a little. Maybe take him to a ball game.

Paul: Cephas is our first-contact specialist, ma'am.

Mrs. Grundy: How interesting. You specialize within the team.

Paul: Yes, ma'am. We each have a specific job description. Cephas plows the ground, as it were. I plant the seed. And Apollos specializes in nurturing and cultivation.

Apollos: God has given each of us a purpose, and our job is the realization of that purpose. When Paul, Cephas, and I work together, the conversion rate is astounding.

Paul: You see, Mrs. Grundy, we work together and do so happily. We don't worry about who takes credit for what conversion. The important thing is that the conversion happens. And God is the one who makes it happen. That's why our motto is . . .

Paul, Apollos, and Cephas: *(raising their hands again)* One for all, and all for the One!

Mrs. Grundy: It sounds just perfect. Why don't more churches use this system?

Paul: Free agents, ma'am.

Mrs. Grundy: I don't understand.

Paul: There are an awful lot of people out there who don't care about the team. Only about their own ego trip. They can't do it all, be all things to all people; and it never occurs to them that they might be more valuable as members of a team than they are alone.

CEPHAS: They don't understand their limitations, so they can't see the benefits of a team approach.

APOLLOS: Most of all, they don't want to share the credit with anyone else.

PAUL: Granted, some free agents do fine work. But too many of them can't carry the ball themselves and fumble, and there's no one there to recover.

APOLLOS: Sadly, it's God's loss.

CEPHAS: Not that we're claiming to be perfect. Far from it. But we try to be aware of our limitations. Each of us does his job, lets God use him to the best of his abilities. The rest we leave in God's hands.

MRS. GRUNDY: I can't think of a better place to be.

PAUL: Glad to hear it. So if we can just get your help in completing this questionnaire, we'll get to work.

(ALL sit down and begin working on a questionnaire.)

NARRATOR: "What, after all, is Apollos? And what is Paul? Only servants, through whom you came to believe — as the Lord has assigned to each his task. I planted the seed, Apollos watered it, but God made it grow. So neither he who plants nor he who waters is anything, but only God, who makes things grow. The man who plants and the man who waters have one purpose, and each will be rewarded according to his own labor. For we are God's fellow workers; you are God's field, God's building."[18]

---

[18] 1 Corinthians 3:5-9

Suing Made Easy

Characters: Herbie, Mary
Costumes: Contemporary

(A bare stage. HERBIE and MARY, children, enter. MARY has her arm around a distraught Herbie.)

MARY: It'll be okay, Herbie. Don't worry. Honest, it'll be okay.

HERBIE: It will not be okay! That was my very last piece of Strawberry Super Double Bubble gum, and I can't buy any more until I get my allowance, which won't be until Thursday.

MARY: That one piece wouldn't have lasted until Thursday.

HERBIE: No, but it would have lasted until supper, except that nasty ol' Mrs. Bradley made me spit it out.

MARY: It's a class rule, Herbie. It's been a class rule a very long time.

HERBIE: It's a stupid rule.

MARY: Maybe, but it's a rule. Have to obey the rules, Herbie, everybody says so.

HERBIE: We don't need rules in Sunday school. Sunday school's for fun. Rules keep you from having fun.

MARY: Rules protect you, Herbie. Like the rule about not running in the hallway. Look what happened to Johnny Rice when he ran in his slick shoes.

HERBIE: *(miming a slip)* Pow! Right into the fire extinguisher!

MARY: I don't think his nose will ever completely unflatten.

HERBIE: My bubble gum wasn't gonna flatten anyone's nose.

MARY: It's still a rule. Mrs. Bradley gets to make the rules, and there's nothing we can do about it.

HERBIE: I could sue her.

MARY: Sue her? What are you talking about?

HERBIE: Don't you watch "Your Turn in Court"?

MARY: Judge Hopner doesn't have time to worry about your bubble gum, Herbie.

HERBIE: Last week, some lady sued this blind man because he stepped on her cat's tail. She wanted lots and lots of money because she had something called "mental anguish" on account of the smushed tail.

MARY: Did she win?

HERBIE: You bet! And Mrs. Bradley isn't even blind. She knew exactly what she had in her hand when she threw my last piece of Strawberry Super Double Bubble gum away.

MARY: I still don't think you can sue, Herbie. I think it's just for grownups.

HERBIE: Kids go see Judge Hopner. A girl sued her brother for snapping the head off her Barbie doll.

MARY: But this is Sunday school, Herbie. We're supposed to love Mrs. Bradley.

HERBIE: I can't love anyone who would take my last piece of Strawberry Super Double Bubble gum. Mary, I want revenge.

MARY: Herbie, I think you're losing control. It was just a piece of gum.

HERBIE: My last piece!

MARY: Until Thursday. It'll take you a year from Thursday just to talk to Judge Hopner. You could talk to Mrs. Bradley right now.

HERBIE: What am I supposed to say? "Gimme back my gum"? I saw it go into the trash.

MARY: And she put it there because kids have been putting gum under the desks and on the floor and in each other's hair. That's why we're not supposed to have gum in Sunday school.

HERBIE: But it was . . .

MARY: I know, your last piece. Tell Mrs. Bradley that. Tell her you're sad. But tell her you're sorry, too.

HERBIE: Okay. *(MARY and HERBIE start to exit.)* But how can I be sure I don't have mental anguish? Is it a rash?

Wish You Were Here

Characters: Gladys, Henry
Costumes: Contemporary

(HENRY is sitting in his easy chair, reading a newspaper. He has a large bandage on his nose. GLADYS enters with a large stack of mail.)

GLADYS: Mail's here, Henry.

HENRY: *(grumpy)* I suppose I got lots of cards again.

GLADYS: You can say that again.

HENRY: Good grief! Why do people insist on sending cards?

GLADYS: *(sarcastically)* They probably have nothing better to do than sit around and think up ways to torment you.

(GLADYS hands him the stack of cards. HENRY looks at the top one.)

HENRY: Just as I suspected. Look at this.

GLADYS: What, dear?

HENRY: Another card from Mrs. Miller. That's the fourth one she's sent me. *(reading card)* "Wish you were here. Hope your nose is mending all right. It's not the same without you."

GLADYS: What a lovely picture on the front.

HENRY: *(reading another card)* And one from Carl Rogers. "We feel like part of us is missing when you're not here." Who are they kidding with all this mushy nonsense?

GLADYS: They're trying to cheer you, Henry.

HENRY: They probably feel guilty. This is all their fault.

GLADYS: How on earth do you figure that?

HENRY: It's the sequence of events. Plain as day. We go to church one Sunday and what happens? The people are nice, friendly. Tell me how happy they are to see me. And I fall for it. Next thing I know I'm accepting invitations to spaghetti dinners, square dances — and a softball game.

GLADYS: Henry, it was not their fault you missed the fly ball.

HENRY: If they hadn't been so friendly, I wouldn't have been in right field in the first place!

GLADYS: Honestly, Henry.

HENRY: *(reading another card)* Listen to this! "Roses are red, guess your nose is, too. At least the ball bounced off your head, and you held the runner to two!"

GLADYS: *(trying not to laugh)* They appreciate you, Henry.

HENRY: *(muttering)* Wish you were here. Hope you feel better. Hurry back. Get well. Why are they doing this to me?

GLADYS: They feel you're a part of them. When you aren't there, it must seem like they're incomplete. Like . . . a body without a nose.

HENRY: Or a wife without a sense of humor.

GLADYS: Henry, they're trying to tell you they miss you. And they need you. What's wrong with that?

HENRY: They want something from me.

GLADYS: Yes, Henry. Your company. Your friendship. They want you to be part of their body again.

HENRY: Really? You think that's all there is to it?

GLADYS: Remember what it says in the Bible? "The body is a unit, though it is made up of many parts; and though all its parts are many, they form one body. So it is with Christ."[19] And so it is with the church. These people love you, Henry—plain and simple. They love you and need you.

HENRY: You're right, Gladys. Why couldn't I see that before?

GLADYS: I don't know, Henry. It's as plain as the nose on your face!

---

[19] 1 Corinthians 12:12

But We've Never Done It This Way

Characters: Narrator, Gloria, Henry, Pastor, James
Costumes: Contemporary

(Chairs are arranged for a small discussion group. GLORIA, HENRY, and JAMES are gathered with their PASTOR.)

NARRATOR: "He has made us competent as ministers of a new covenant — not of the letter but of the Spirit; for the letter kills, but the Spirit gives life."[20]

GLORIA: Pastor, I have to be honest with you. What happened Sunday morning . . . I wasn't comfortable with it. And I wasn't the only one. Several people made a point of telling me how unhappy they were.

HENRY: You threw a lot of people for a loop there, Pastor.

PASTOR: Are you referring to my inviting those with ailments or specific needs to come forward for a time of special prayer?

GLORIA: Yes. That's it exactly.

PASTOR: What I did comes straight from the New Testament.

GLORIA: That's fine, Pastor, but it's not the way we do things around here.

JAMES: We're regular people, Pastor, used to a regular way of doing things. A routine. Lets people feel at home, like part of the family.

PASTOR: But your family is thinning out, James. When I was called to be your pastor, I was given a mandate to revive an ailing church, a church that was losing members rapidly. Your membership has dropped by half in the last twenty years. Of the half that remains, a third are homebound or spend six months of the year in Florida. I thought I was empowered to do what was necessary to breathe life back into a dead horse.

GLORIA: Don't you call my church a dead horse.

PASTOR: How about a terminally ill one?

GLORIA: Pastor! I am not amused.

PASTOR: Neither am I, Gloria. Frankly, I'm losing my patience with the attitudes around here. How am I supposed to fix the problem if you people pitch a fit anytime I try something new?

JAMES: We don't have a problem with trying new things.

PASTOR: Really? When was the last time you let someone change something around here?

(Pause as GLORIA, JAMES, and HENRY think hard.)

HENRY: We got new hymnals a couple of years back.

PASTOR: A couple of years back? Henry, those hymnals were purchased in 1969. But I guess it's all relative after a while, isn't it?

JAMES: Like we told you, people are comfortable with things the way they are. People can't be expected to up and change overnight.

PASTOR: That's not what I expect. I'd just like to see a few open minds when I do something like inviting people forward to pray.

GLORIA: But Pastor, don't you see? It makes us look like one of those churches.

PASTOR: What do you mean by "one of those churches"?

GLORIA: Those frivolous little places that are doing something new every week, that have no appreciation for tradition and ritual.

---

[20] 2 Corinthians 3:6

PASTOR: I'm all for tradition, Gloria, but how am I supposed to invite new members into the congregation when you people act like you inherited your pews? You all sit in the same place, talk to the same people, and leave by the same door every single Sunday. You make new people feel about as welcome as fleas at a dog show.

GLORIA: Pastor!

JAMES: Don't you get it, Pastor? We've always done it this way.

PASTOR: And that makes it the right way?

GLORIA: Change is scary — too scary.

PASTOR: But Gloria, change is exactly what the gospel challenges us to do. Change. Grow. Learn.

HENRY: I knew he was going to drag the gospel into it sooner or later.

JAMES: Actually, Pastor has a point there.

GLORIA: I don't know what church you think you're going to, James, but it won't work here. Our congregation won't put up with these radical new ideas. If we don't stop him now, James, he'll have people dancing in the aisles before you know it.

PASTOR: Dancing in the aisles! What a great idea for Palm Sunday!

GLORIA: *(standing)* Hear that? Just what I was afraid of. I won't be any part of this change nonsense. I'm staying true to the old ways.

(GLORIA leaves in a huff. The men watch her go.)

PASTOR: If she's right about this congregation, maybe I should be the one to leave.

HENRY: Yup. You leave, and then we call some other young fellow with bright ideas; and he leaves, and we call another — and on and on and on. We've always done it this way, Pastor.

Lifestyles of the Not-So-Rich and Famous

Characters: Robin, Paul
Costumes: Contemporary

(ROBIN, garishly dressed, rushes out to center stage with a microphone in his hand. He plays to an unseen camera crew.)

ROBIN: Good morning! Welcome to another edition of "Lifestyles of the Not-So-Rich and Famous." I'm your host, Robin Screech, and this week we're going to be looking at a person whose eternal smile caught our camera's eye. A person who seems to truly enjoy life to the fullest. Our secret undercover reporter followed this person around town for several days and was amazed at the constant level of joy he displayed. He goes simply by the name Paul, and we're here in the sun-drenched Greek city of Corinth to discover the secret to his wonderful life. Here he comes now.

(PAUL, modestly dressed, enters and starts to walk right by Robin. ROBIN gestures to the camera crew to follow him as he intercepts Paul.)

ROBIN *(CONT)*: Good morning, friend.

PAUL: Good morning.

ROBIN: Are you the happy fellow they call Paul?

PAUL: I'm known as Paul, yes.

ROBIN: Paul, I'm Robin Screech, and as a portion of my television show *(gestures to camera crew)*, I'd like to talk to you about your interesting lifestyle.

PAUL: It's easy enough to explain. I'm following Christ's example; I'm taking up my cross and following him.

ROBIN: Sorry? Not sure I caught that.

PAUL: As I tell my friends here in Corinth, "You're not your own; Christ paid a great price for you."

ROBIN: So here we have a glimpse into the source of this man's happiness. Wealth so vast he can buy friends.

PAUL: That's not what I'm saying at all. What I'm saying is, all I have isn't mine. It's the Lord's.

ROBIN: And which Lord would that be, Paul? Are you related to nobility, or is it a business relationship? How exactly do you finance your yacht, your summer home, your Rolls Royce?

PAUL: Robin, if I had any of those things, they too would be the Lord's. But I don't have any of those things.

ROBIN: Paul, how can you expect our viewers to believe that you have no vast wealth, no material possessions, and yet you walk around all day with a huge smile and a kind word for everyone?

PAUL: My joy is in Christ. "To live is Christ and to die is gain."[21] What better treasure could there be than Jesus Christ, our Savior?

ROBIN: *(to camera crew)* Who did the research on this guy?

PAUL: Robin, let me tell you what I told my good friend Timothy . . .

ROBIN: The stations would rather rerun Captain Kangaroo than show this moron.

---

[21]Philippians 1:21

PAUL: I told Timothy, "The love of money is a root of all kinds of evil."[22] Money, cars, material wealth, it all has the same effect.

ROBIN: You can't say that on my show. I have a credit card company as a sponsor.

PAUL: Some people, eager for wealth, have wandered from the faith and paid a terrible price.

ROBIN: *(giving the cut sign)* All right. We can't save this one. Cut.

PAUL: *(taking the microphone)* Tell me something about yourself, Robin. Do you know the Lord Jesus Christ?

ROBIN: *(to crew)* I said cut!

---

[22] 1 Timothy 6:10

Pennies for Heaven

Characters: Boy, Girl
Costumes: Contemporary

(A young Boy sits in the center of the stage. He is counting pennies out of a pile into a dish. As he counts, a young Girl enters.)

Boy: Eighty-three, eighty-four, eighty-five . . .

Girl: Whatcha doing?

Boy: Counting my pennies.

Girl: Looks like you have a lot of them.

Boy: Pretty many.

Girl: Are you saving for something special?

Boy: You bet.

Girl: A toy? A game? A bicycle, maybe?

Boy: No, nothing like that. I'm going to give my pennies to the church.

Girl: That's boring.

Boy: No, it's not. It's exciting. See, every year my church takes a special offering for a project called Reach Out for Christ. The money goes to kids all over the country who don't have it as good as we do.

Girl: I don't have it so good. I want my own phone and my own TV, and my mom says I can't have them.

Boy: Yeah, but you have a mom and dad. A lot of these kids don't even have that. Some of my pennies will go to kids in Oklahoma and the people who take care of them because they don't have moms and dads.

Girl: But you don't know those kids in Oklahoma. Wouldn't you rather spend the money on yourself? Or on me?

Boy: Nope. I have to do my Christian responsibility.

Girl: I don't think I have one of those, either.

Boy: Sure you do. We all do. If I understand my dad right, Christian responsibility means taking what God gives you and sharing it with others.

Girl: Sounds like you're doing a lot of giving away. What are you getting?

Boy: I'm getting a wonderful feeling. You know how you feel when you first turn the lights on, on the Christmas tree? Or how you feel when you see a rainbow? That feeling like your heart's all full of sunshine?

Girl: *(nodding)* It's wonderful.

Boy: Well, that's the feeling I get when I put my pennies in the offering.

Girl: Wow. Could I put some pennies in, too?

Boy: Sure!

(The Girl digs into her pocket and drops pennies, one by one, into the bowl.)

Boy *(cont)*: Eighty-six, eighty-seven, eighty-eight.

(They look at each other and smile.)

Jones, Jones, and Jones

Characters: Narrator, Philip, Receptionist
Costumes: Contemporary

(The reception area of an office suite. The RECEPTIONIST sits behind a desk, answering a phone.)

NARRATOR: "There is neither Jew nor Greek, slave nor free, male nor female, for you are all one in Christ Jesus."[23]

(PHILIP enters. He looks around nervously and relaxes when he notes he is the only visitor. He approaches the Receptionist.)

PHILIP: Hello. I'd like to talk to the pastor about a problem I have.

RECEPTIONIST: Of course, sir. Is the problem personal or theological?

PHILIP: I'd say it's personal.

RECEPTIONIST: Well, sir, we have three pastors, all well-trained and willing to offer counseling.

PHILIP: Three? I didn't realize I had a choice.

RECEPTIONIST: Certainly. Would you like to see Pastor Jones, Pastor Jones, or Pastor Jones?

PHILIP: Miss, I don't have time to play games.

RECEPTIONIST: I understand that, sir. If you'll just tell me if you want to see Pastor Jones, Pastor Jones, or Pastor Jones we can get you an appointment right away.

PHILIP: You have three pastors, all with the same last name?

RECEPTIONIST: Yes, sir.

PHILIP: How am I supposed to choose? Look, let me talk to the senior pastor.

RECEPTIONIST: They are co-pastors, sir.

PHILIP: Okay. Who has the final say in things?

RECEPTIONIST: They have equal say in all things, sir.

PHILIP: Well, which one is most qualified to deal with personal problems?

RECEPTIONIST: They are equally well-qualified, sir. Each one has a complete seminary education and is ordained. Each has clinical pastoral experience. Each is equally involved in the pulpit ministry of this church. *(smiling)* We're kinda big on equality around here, sir.

PHILIP: There must be something that distinguishes one from the other.

RECEPTIONIST: Trivial things, perhaps. Nothing important.

PHILIP: What do you consider trivial?

RECEPTIONIST: Race, gender, things like that.

PHILIP: You mean to tell me that one of these pastors is a woman?

RECEPTIONIST: No, sir.

PHILIP: Whew. That's a relief.

RECEPTIONIST: One of them is a man.

PHILIP: You have two female pastors?

RECEPTIONIST: We're all one in Christ Jesus, sir. Like I said before, our pastors are all of equal ability and wisdom. If you're having difficulty making a choice, perhaps I can help you. But I'll need to know a little bit about your problem.

PHILIP: I'm closed-minded.

RECEPTIONIST: Closed-minded?

PHILIP: I tend not to accept new ideas, change, or people in atypical roles.

---

[23]Galatians 3:28

RECEPTIONIST: Like women as pastors.

PHILIP: Look, it's nothing against women, really. I've just always regarded the white, Anglo-Saxon male as a superior being, and I have trouble accepting that I should think any differently. Now I have a new boss. He's Hispanic. It just doesn't seem right. I'm having a rough time.

RECEPTIONIST: Have you thought about why you feel this way?

PHILIP: Sure. Look at any map and it's as plan as day. Where's the old U.S. of A.? Smack dab in the middle of things. Central and South America are below us, so's Africa. Everything else is shoved to the sides, except Canada—which always has thought way too highly of itself, so it makes sense they're floating around up top. But America? Top of the heap. Where it belongs. Because it's full of white, Anglo-Saxon Protestants like me. So you're going to ask me to work for some Hispanic guy from Mexico?

RECEPTIONIST: Have you considered that where your boss comes from isn't important at all? That what counts is that we're all one in Christ? All equal in the eyes of the Lord?

PHILIP: I tried to think about it once or twice, but I couldn't bring myself to accept it. I could just feel my mind closing up.

RECEPTIONIST: Have you talked to your wife about this?

PHILIP: I'm not married. Almost made the fatal trip down the aisle once, but she was too closed-minded about having children—didn't want more than two, and I have to have at least eight. She wouldn't come around to my way of thinking, so I told her to forget it.

RECEPTIONIST: I'm sorry.

PHILIP: I'm not. Women. Anyway, you better let me see this man pastor. Maybe he'll understand where I'm coming from.

RECEPTIONIST: Okay. Let me just buzz José and see if he's free.

PHILIP: José? Pastor José Jones?

RECEPTIONIST: Yes. I think you'll like him a lot. He's very warm. And open-minded.

PHILIP: *(looking at his watch)* Gosh, look at the time. I have . . . a dentist appointment. Yes. Dentist. Gotta run. Thanks for your help.

(PHILIP rushes out. The RECEPTIONIST calls after him.)

RECEPTIONIST: You're always welcome to come back. And we'll always be happy to see you— as an equal!

Landing on Boardwalk

Characters: Lynn, Pat, Lou
Costumes: Contemporary

(LYNN, PAT, and LOU sit around a table, playing Monopoly. The box top is propped up against the table so the audience can see it.)

LYNN: All right! You landed on Connecticut Avenue, Pat. Guess who owns it — and the hotel that's built smack dab in the middle! That'll be six hundred dollars, babe. Pay up.

PAT: Six hundred dollars? Really?

LYNN: You got it. And I want it. A big fat six with two nice, round zeroes after it.

(LYNN holds out her hand, and PAT counts the bills into it.)

PAT: One, two, three, four, five, five-fifty, five-sixty, five-eighty, six hundred.

LYNN: *(fanning the bills)* I love it, I love it. Roll, Lou, what're you waiting for?

LOU: *(rolling)* Eight. *(moving token)* Six, seven, eight.

LYNN: Well would you look at that? New York Avenue. And what a pretty hotel. One thousand dollars, please.

LOU: Oh, no.

LYNN: Oh, yes. You play, you pay. Fork it over, Lou. Every last cent.

LOU: Mellow out, Lynn. You don't have to be so greedy.

LYNN: I'm not being greedy. I'm showing my enthusiasm for the game. Now gimme what you owe me.

LOU: *(handing over the money)* Okay, okay. Don't spend it all in one place.

LYNN: What are you so down about? You rolled doubles. Go again.

LOU: *(rolling)* Ten. *(moving token)* Which means . . .

LYNN: *(bouncing in excitement)* Yes! Yes! Marvin Gardens! And yet another in my lovely line of hotels. For a grand total of $1275. Payable right this very minute.

LOU: Great. *(counting out bills)* There you go. Happy?

LYNN: And getting happier all the time. Unlike you two sourpusses. Go on, Lou. You got doubles again. Roll, roll, roll.

LOU: I can't wait. *(rolling)* Eight. *(moving token)* Oh, no. Park Place.

LYNN: Oh, baby, you're in for it now. Go for it, Pat.

LOU: Guess you're entitled to your piece of the shrinking pie, Pat. How much do I owe you?

PAT: Nothing, Lou. You're almost tapped out. We'll let it go this time.

LOU: Thanks, Pat. That's great.

LYNN: Excuse me. Are we or are we not playing by the rules here? Lou landed on your property, Pat, and you have an obligation to take every cent Lou's got.

PAT: I choose not to, Lynn.

LYNN: That's not a choice you can make. That's not what the game is all about.

LOU: Pat's letting me stay in the game by giving me a break, Lynn. Pat's demonstrating grace. Are you familiar with the term?

LYNN: Look, are we gonna play, or are we gonna talk? If you two want to be all wimpy and sweet with each other, that's your business. But I'm here to play. So let's do it. *(rolling)* Seven! *(moving token)* Chance. Better be a good one. *(selecting card)* Advance to Boardwalk. Oh no! Who's got Boardwalk — with two hotels! That's two thousand dollars!

PAT: No, that's four thousand dollars. Remember? We agreed to play by your special rules, which allow two hotels on each property and double the rental price.

LYNN: Four thousand. That cleans me out! I'm ruined. Stomped. Destroyed.

PAT: It's all right, Lynn. I'll let it go.

LYNN: What?

PAT: I don't want to end the game. I'll show you the same courtesy I showed Lou. Forget your debt. Let's keep playing.

(LYNN bolts to her feet.)

LYNN: If you think I'm going to play for another minute with the two of you, who obviously don't understand the point of playing in the first place, you're mistaken. If you can't be ruthless and cold when the game demands it, who needs you?

(LYNN storms off.)

LOU: Brings a whole new meaning to the word "graceless," doesn't it?

PAT: There but for the grace of God go a lot of us. *(handing Lou the dice)* I think it's your roll, Lou.

Season with Salt

Characters: Beth, Bob
Costumes: Contemporary

(BETH enters. BOB trudges wearily behind her. BETH stops and turns to watch him catch up with her. BOB looks at her with a discouraged frown.)

BOB: I'll never be a good witness, Beth. Never ever in a million years. Witnessing is the worst.

BETH: Bob, you're being a little melodramatic, aren't you?

BOB: Yeah? How many souls have I brought to Jesus since I started evangelizing? *(gestures)* Zippo.

BETH: Well, maybe you need to adjust your approach.

BOB: *(wry)* What could be wrong with my approach? I tell a person about Jesus, and they look at me like I'm a cheesecake.

BETH: Fruitcake.

BOB: That too. Why can't I lead whole flocks of souls to the Lord like Pastor Lemaster on TV?

BETH: Because you aren't Pastor Lemaster on TV.

BOB: I know that, Beth. But I ordered his videotape—"Seven Sure-fire Threats to Bring Your Friends to Christ," a dynamic introduction to foolproof conversion presented on one specially priced videocassette. And I studied the tape, and I did the companion workbook . . .

BETH: Bob, just show me.

BOB: Show you what?

BETH: Show me what you do.

BOB: Well, I sit in front of the TV and hold the VCR remote in my right hand . . .

BETH: No, Bob. Show me what you do when you approach someone to witness.

(BOB looks around nervously.)

BOB: Here? Now?

BETH: Aren't you prepared to witness anywhere, anytime?

BOB: Yeah, but . . .

BETH: C'mon. Pretend I'm a no-good pagan who needs to know Christ.

(BOB looks at her suspiciously for a moment then shrugs. He takes a deep breath, runs his hands through his hair, shakes his hands loose, and stomps a foot.)

BOB: *(roaring)* "Miss, do you know Jesus as your personal savior? Do you realize that if you died tonight, you'd be roasting in the fires of hell like a pig on a spit over a hot, open fire? Are you willing to be fried like a chicken, or would you like to accept Christ as your Lord and Savior?"

BETH: *(pause)* I see.

BOB: I'm too soft in my approach, aren't I? Maybe I should put some more blood and guts into it.

BETH: No, no, no. I don't think that's the problem at all.

BOB: Great. So it's me. I just don't have the Pastor Lemaster fire-and-brimstone blessing from the Almighty.

BETH: Bob, it's not you. It's your . . . approach. Have you considered being natural? being yourself?

BOB: Well . . . no.

BETH: Why do you need to become a different person to share something so very personal?

Bob: Well . . . "if we are to reach those lost souls on the brink of damnation . . ."

Beth: Bob! That's not you talking, that's Pastor Lemaster. Talk from the heart — your own heart.

Bob: I'm too bland.

Beth: No, you're not. You may not be a big bag of exotic spices, but you're the salt of the earth. And that makes you well seasoned. Your message should be seasoned the same way. Make the dish appealing. Do you like Brussels sprouts?

Bob: Yuck. The worst. But my mom told me I had to eat them or I wouldn't get enough vitamin K and my hair would fall out.

Beth: So you ate them out of fear. And you never bothered to notice whether they might have a wonderful flavor all their own.

Bob: Wait . . . so if people come to Jesus out of fear, they'll never know his true nature?

Beth: People who are worried about "frying like a chicken" are going to be too preoccupied to hear the message of love and grace that the Lord truly offers.

Bob: Yeah, but still . . . You're asking me to open up to people I don't know, to share my heart with strangers.

Beth: If you have to hide behind someone else's mask to talk about your relationship with the Lord, maybe that relationship needs work.

Bob: *(considering)* Or maybe it just needs a little less pepper.

(They smile and embrace.)

Labor Pains

Characters: Husband, Wife
Costumes: Contemporary

(The WIFE, very, very pregnant, is easing herself into a chair. A suitcase sits next to the chair. HUSBAND enters, carrying a briefcase.)

HUSBAND: Hi, honey, I'm home! How ya doing?

(HUSBAND kisses her perfunctorily, then goes to take his coat off.)

WIFE: Oh, it's been an *(wince)* interesting day.

HUSBAND: Great. When's dinner? The game starts in about an hour. Are we gonna make it?

WIFE: *(another wince)* When you say "Are we gonna make it?" what exactly do you mean, sweetheart?

HUSBAND: Hey, babe, what's with the funny faces? Is the baby doing somersaults or something?

WIFE: I would say it's in the "or something" category. Honey, I think it's time.

HUSBAND: For dinner? Great. I'm starved.

WIFE: Not dinner, dear. Time for the baby.

HUSBAND: Go on. The baby's not due for another two weeks.

WIFE: Darling, I don't care when it's due. It's coming now.

HUSBAND: It's probably false labor. Have you been eating spicy foods today?

WIFE: Dear, stop arguing and go get the car.

HUSBAND: I'm not arguing. I'm just trying to be rational. The baby is not due. We haven't had dinner. And there's a great game on tonight. Why on earth should we be having a baby at a time like this? We planned this baby down to the last detail. How can it possibly be early? You know I don't like surprises. I like things to happen according to schedule.

WIFE: You explain that to our child when he or she arrives. But when he or she arrives, I would prefer for it to be in a hospital, not here on the living-room floor. I know we've made a lot of plans, but it seems God is operating off another set of blueprints, dear. Let's go.

HUSBAND: God wouldn't do this to me. God knows I don't like disruptions. God knows the crib isn't here yet, we haven't chosen a diaper service, and I still want to wallpaper the nursery.

WIFE: God knows what's best, dear. Including what's best for this baby. And if what's best is to be born tonight, I'm not going to argue — with the baby or with God. And neither are you! Let's go!

HUSBAND: I can't believe that God, who was organized enough to create the world in six days, would do this to me. How can God throw something like this at me when I'm not prepared? I'm not ready!

WIFE: I am!

HUSBAND: Okay, okay. *(They start out.)* Can we watch the game in the delivery room? Honey?

The Reverend Maximillion Finley

Characters: Teresa, Rob, Maximillion
Costumes: Contemporary

(TERESA and ROB wait in the lobby of an auditorium. An easel behind them proclaims, "TO-NIGHT ONLY! REVEREND MAXIMILLION FINLEY IN PERSON!" TERESA clutches an autograph book and looks around excitedly. ROB is subdued.)

TERESA: This is so exciting. I can barely stand it.

ROB: Teresa, he's a flashy showman — the gospel according to Liberace.

TERESA: Rob! How can you talk about the Reverend Maximillion Finley that way? He's a great man of immense spiritual gifts. He's the real thing.

ROB: I thought Coke had that market locked.

TERESA: Don't make jokes. Maximillion is a modern-day prophet. A contemporary Abraham. A Malachi for our times.

ROB: Malachi?

TERESA: Malachi's the one who said, "Bring the whole tithe into the storehouse."[24] Reverend Maximillion has revamped that message, so that it's relevant for our lives today. Maximillion says, "Put a whole lot of car in your garage."

ROB: Sorry, I seem to be missing the relevance of that one.

TERESA: The Reverend wants us to have faith. We shouldn't drive those dinky, little subcompacts. We should trust God and buy one of those big, beautiful luxury cars.

ROB: What in the world is the connection between a Lincoln Continental and Malachi?

TERESA: Quiet! I think he's coming! Oh, look! There he is! I'm so excited!

(MAXIMILLION appears. He is the Las Vegas-floor-show version of a preacher — loud with flashy clothes and a similar manner. TERESA rushes up to him, autograph book extended.)

TERESA (CONT): Oh, Reverend Maximillion, may I have your autograph? I'm such a devoted fan — follower — of yours.

MAXIMILLION: *(taking the autograph book)* Well, praise the Lord! Sing hallelujah! Amen! Amen! It's such a pleasure to see the pretty, young sisters hearing the message and responding with such enthusiasm.

(MAXIMILLION signs the book with a flourish and returns it to Teresa.)

TERESA: Oh, yes, sir. Thank you, sir.

MAXIMILLION: It warms the very depths of my soul to see people getting excited about the positive news of our good and gracious Lord. I get excited when they realize the truth — God doesn't want us to wait in the soup line, God wants us to be in the steak line!

TERESA: Hallelujah!

MAXIMILLION: God isn't calling us to the dime store. He's not even calling us to Kmart. God is calling us to Neiman Marcus, and we should pay full price!

TERESA: Oh, it's true. It is so true.

MAXIMILLION: Sister, I sense that you are a woman of deep faith. That's why I am going to present you with this special, personalized, Reverend Maximillion Finley discount coupon. *(handing her the coupon)* Right now, God bless us, we're offering a limited-edition "Sweat of My Brow" commemorative. We will send you, to cherish in the privacy of your own home, a handkerchief with which I have wiped the sweat from my brow during a sermon. Praise God, this simple square of 100 percent Irish linen

---

[24]Malachi 3:10

will bring healing to your life. Hallelujah, it can cure arthritis. Praise Jesus, it can calm indigestion. And we're asking people to send in a mere one-hundred dollars for the great blessing of this "Sweat of My Brow" artifact. But if you use that coupon, you can get the blessed hanky for half the price. Praise his name!

ROB: *(stepping forward)* You can't be serious.

MAXIMILLION: I realize it seems silly for me to be offering so much for so little, but the Spirit is filling my heart and telling me that this sister is special.

TERESA: Thank you, Reverend Maximillion. Thank you.

ROB: Teresa, you aren't really falling for this junk, are you?

MAXIMILLION: Do I detect . . . unbelief?

ROB: No, you detect common sense. I can't believe you expect people to fall for this hokey routine.

TERESA: Rob!

ROB: Don't "Rob!" me. He's the one who's robbing you.

MAXIMILLION: The Lord loves a cheerful giver, son. Praise the name of Jesus!

ROB: How does he feel about greedy takers?

TERESA: Rob, please.

MAXIMILLION: It's obvious that Satan has closed your eyes to the truth.

ROB: No, the Lord has opened my eyes — and I see a crook. Wasn't it the apostle Paul who said, "For the love of money is a root of all kinds of evil. Some people, eager for money, have wandered from the faith and pierced themselves with many griefs"?[25]

MAXIMILLION: That's an old translation.

ROB: Oh? Has it changed much in the new version?

MAXIMILLION: My translation says, "The lack of money is the root of all evil."

ROB: Is that based on the original Greek?

MAXIMILLION: It's based on a personal revelation I received from the Lord God Almighty, blessed be the name of God.

ROB: Excuse me. I'm receiving a revelation of my own. And I'm outta here.

(ROB starts to exit. TERESA grabs his arm.)

TERESA: Rob, you can't leave now. I think we're onto some great truths here.

ROB: All that I'm onto is the scam your flashy friend here is running. You want to buy into it, go ahead. But buying is all you're doing, remember that.

(ROB exits. TERESA turns back to Maximillion.)

TERESA: Forgive him, Reverend Maximillion. He's having trouble dealing with all this new information.

MAXIMILLION: Some people have trouble with the truth, sister, and we must be compassionate. I'm just glad I can count on your support. In fact, your support means so much to me that I want you to have another discount coupon. *(handing it to her)* Now you can order our brand-new "John the Baptist in the Desert" terrarium and get it at the low, low price of $49.95. Blessings are just raining down on you, sister.

TERESA: Thank you, Reverend Maximillion. Bless you.

MAXIMILLION: Blessings right back at you, sister. Go in peace. Shop well.

(MAXIMILLION exits. TERESA looks after him adoringly.)

TERESA: A handkerchief and a terrarium. Imagine. Who says you can't buy happiness?

---

[25] 1 Timothy 6:10

Rummage Sale

Characters: June, Andrea, Shoppers (non-speaking)
Costumes: Contemporary

(SHOPPERS are working their way through several tables filled with junk. A poster proclaims "CHURCH RUMMAGE SALE." JUNE waves across several tables to ANDREA. They cross to meet.)

JUNE: Andrea, I can't believe some of this stuff that you're selling.

ANDREA: Just trying to lighten the ship so it will sail faster, as it were.

JUNE: I thought this church never threw out anything. *(pointing)* What's in that box?

ANDREA: Oh, it's the T-shirt lost and found. Seems every time we have a youth retreat or lock-in, we wind up with T-shirts left behind.

JUNE: You think people are going to buy them?

ANDREA: June, people will buy anything at a rummage sale. Look at that man over there. He's going to buy that whole box of candle stubs from the Christmas Eve candlelight service. To you and me it's a box of wax fragments, but to him it's a treasure.

JUNE: *(pointing again)* And you're selling Bibles?

ANDREA: Unclaimed ones. People leave them behind at services and classes all the time, then never come back and claim them. I'd rather sell them than leave them in the church office. You never know who might buy one on a whim and discover a real treasure.

JUNE: True. But what about those books? *(pointing)* It looks like you're selling the whole church library.

ANDREA: No, those are books people have donated to us. We give some to our shut-ins and take some to the hospital, but more come in all the time. Whenever members clean out their attics, we seem to get the leftovers.

JUNE: Wait. *(picking up a small box)* Don't tell me you're selling offering envelopes?

ANDREA: *(shrugging)* Maybe someone can find another use for them. These pledge envelopes were never picked up.

JUNE: This carton is almost full. We must have a lot of people who aren't using their envelopes.

ANDREA: And they aren't throwing their money into the plate naked, either, June.

JUNE: Why are people so eager to buy junk—in fact, they'll stand in line to do it—but when it comes to paying for something truly precious, they run away?

ANDREA: People put value on the things they have to struggle for—things they have to dig in dusty boxes or stand in line for. But things that are there in the open, ready for the taking, they ignore. If they can't put a value on it, they can't imagine paying for it.

JUNE: Miss some real bargains that way.

ANDREA: Speaking of bargains, look at that. *(pointing)* That woman is going to buy the old coffee pot from the fellowship hall.

JUNE: She's obviously not a member here. Otherwise, she'd know the kind of coffee that pot makes!

(JUNE and ANDREA laugh.)

Believe It or Not

Characters: Randall, Abe, Stage Manager, Mrs. Edison, Tim, Nellie
Costumes: Contemporary

(A living room. RANDALL enters, having just returned home from work. He sits down in an armchair with a grateful sigh and closes his eyes. ABE leaps up from behind the couch and speaks into a hand-held microphone.)

ABE: Mr. Randall Hughes, believe it or not! *(RANDALL jumps.)* You are the guest star of tonight's episode of the TV craze that's sweeping the nation—"America's Believe It or Not!"

(The STAGE MANAGER steps in from the wings and shows the audience an APPLAUSE sign. He waits impassively for the audience reaction, then steps offstage again. ABE steps out from behind the couch and approaches Randall.)

ABE *(CONT)*: I'm Abe Abraham, your host for tonight's exciting, penetrating, and occasionally meaningful examination of those important issues people just don't discuss often enough these days—believe it or not!

(STAGE MANAGER shows the applause sign.)

ABE *(CONT)*: Tonight, we've invaded the home of Mr. Randall Hughes. Mr. Hughes, say hello to the folks at home.

RANDALL: Who let you in here?

ABE: I'll pay for the broken window, Mr. Hughes. Just relax, and tell our audience what you do for a living.

RANDALL: I'm a vice president for . . .

ABE: No brand names, sir.

RANDALL: A major restaurant-supply company.

ABE: Wow. Sounds pretty darn impressive to me.

RANDALL: I make a good living.

ABE: Would you classify yourself as a man of faith?

RANDALL: You mean religion and that stuff?

ABE: Exactly.

RANDALL: I'd say I'm as religious as the next guy.

ABE: Mr. Hughes, you were raised in a Christian home. Your mother and father participated in the activities of the local church. You grew up in a Sunday school program that taught you all about the wonderful biblical heroes. But something happened when you turned twelve. Do you remember, Randall?

MRS. EDISON: *(offstage)* I remember saying to Randy, "You've never accepted Jesus as your Savior, have you?" And he looked me square in the eye and said, "When I see him, I'll believe in him."

ABE: Randall, that voice—believe it or not—is the voice of Mrs. Theo Edison, your sixth-grade Sunday school teacher! Come on out, Mrs. Edison!

(STAGE MANAGER shows applause sign as MRS. EDISON enters. She hugs the bewildered Randall.)

ABE *(CONT)*: Mrs. Edison, that moment must have been difficult for you. Can you tell us what was going through your mind as this vulnerable young boy declared his disbelief?

MRS. EDISON: I prayed. I prayed that someday Jesus would be made real to Randy. I understand that sometimes we're called to simply plant the seeds, while others reap the harvest. I did what I could.

(MRS. EDISON goes to the couch and sits down. RANDALL is stunned.)

ABE: Well, Mrs. Edison, the little Randy you knew has grown up to be, in his own words, "just as religious as the next guy." But let's not get ahead of ourselves. Let's look at your college days, Randall, and recall the afternoon you met — this fellow.

TIM: *(offstage)* I was in my dorm room, reading my Bible, and my roommate came in with Randy. Randy noticed my Bible and looked at me oddly. I asked him if he had read the Good Book, and he said, "A little, as a kid." So I asked him why he didn't read it anymore. He said, "I believe in the here and now, the things I'm sure of, not a bunch of stories about people I can't see."

ABE: That's right, Randall. That's the voice — believe it or not — of Tim Thomas, now an honest and respected Christian businessman, a fellow you considered an oddball in college. Tim, come on out and say "Hi" to Randall.

(STAGE MANAGER shows sign. TIM enters and shakes Randall's hand. RANDALL is growing more and more perplexed.)

ABE: Any other thoughts about Randall you'd like to share with us, Tim?

TIM: Not really. Whenever I saw Randall after that encounter, he would avoid me.

(TIM goes to sit with Mrs. Edison.)

RANDALL: Wait a minute here. I've had enough of this. What are you people up to, anyway?

ABE: You're about to see, Randall. There's just one more person we want you to meet.

NELLIE: *(offstage)* I was Mr. Hughes' secretary for three years. As a committed Christian, I often read my Bible and prayed during my lunch breaks. Mr. Hughes told me I should keep my religion at home. I asked his permission to take a long lunch to attend Good Friday services, and he said no.

ABE: You know her as Mrs. Smith, Randall, but to friends and family, she's just plain Nellie. Believe it or not, here's Nellie Smith.

(STAGE MANAGER shows sign. NELLIE enters. She politely shakes hands with Randall.)

ABE *(CONT)*: Nellie, any thoughts on Mr. Hughes' problem?

NELLIE: I think it's a simple lack of faith, resulting in a loss of hope. If he can't see it, he can't be bothered with it. He has no room in his life for uncertainty. He's always been the sort of person who only reacts to facts and figures.

ABE: Excellent analysis.

(NELLIE joins the others on the couch.)

RANDALL: All right, all right. I believe. If it's so important to all of you, I believe.

ABE: Really? And has that belief made an impact on your life, Randall?

RANDALL: I guess so. If that's part of it.

ABE: What impact might that be?

RANDALL: I . . . Nothing comes to mind, but you've caught me unprepared.

ABE: You should have thought of that when you chose not to believe. You don't do you, Randall?

RANDALL: *(quietly)* No.

ABE: Okay, folks, that's a wrap.

(NELLIE, TIM, and MRS. EDISON file out. The STAGE MANAGER comes out and takes Abe's microphone. ABE starts to leave, but RANDALL grabs him.)

RANDALL: Wait. Is that it? Is that all there is?

ABE: *(nodding slowly)* Yep. It all comes down to a simple decision — believe it or not.

Long Distance Sprinting

Characters: Al, Phil
Costumes: Contemporary

(Al sits in his armchair, reading the newspaper. There is a knock at the door.)
Al: Come in! Door's open.
(Phil enters.)
Phil: Hi, Al.
Al: Hey, Phil. What brings you by?
Phil: Burn out.
Al: What are you burned out on?
Phil: Church. I've had it. I can't take anymore.
Al: Phil, I don't understand. You committed your life to Christ three years ago. I thought these had been three great years. How can you be burned out on salvation?
Phil: Oh, the salvation part's fine, but I can't keep up with all these demands anymore.
Al: What demands?
Phil: Let me sketch it out for you. I had a board meeting Monday night, small-group Bible study Tuesday night, prayer meeting Wednesday, visitation Thursday; I chaperoned youth-group roller-skating Friday, and hosted the men's breakfast at church Saturday morning. By Saturday night the thought of going back to church to worship Sunday morning was too much for me. I didn't have the energy to even think about participating in a worship service. I can't go on, Al. I feel like a long-distance runner who's been sprinting the whole race.
Al: Phil, take it easy. I believe you're tired — and you have a right to be. But why are you taking on so many things at once?
Phil: I'm just trying to do what the Bible teaches.
Al: What lesson is that?
Phil: Hebrews 12:1-3. I have it memorized, because I led a discussion on it in small-group Bible study last week. "Therefore, since we are surrounded by such a great cloud of witnesses, let us throw off everything that hinders and the sin that so easily entangles, and let us run with perseverance the race marked out for us. Let us fix our eyes on Jesus, the author and perfecter of our faith, who for the joy set before him endured the cross, scorning its shame, and sat down at the right hand of the throne of God. Consider him who endured such opposition from sinful men, so that you will not grow weary and lose heart." Did you catch that last part? "So you will not grow weary"? Too late. I'm beat.
Al: So am I, just from listening to you. How did you memorize all that?
Phil: Al, I need some help.
Al: Phil, those verses don't say that you have to do something church related in every spare moment of your time. They're talking about an attitude, a mind-set. They're talking about defining a lifestyle.
Phil: You sound like a Weight Watchers ad.
Al: Phil, those verses are talking about living to glorify Jesus. Letting your light shine so that people know you're a Christian.
Phil: I've sure shown my neighbor I'm a Christian. Three nights in a row, he's invited me over to share homemade ice cream with his family, and each time I've had to say no because I'm rushing off to some church function or another.

AL: My point exactly. Maybe you'd be doing more for the kingdom by sharing ice cream—and your witness—with your neighbor than you're able to do in three board meetings. Besides, if you're always racing around looking harried because of church, how attractive does that make our church look to others?

PHIL: I hadn't thought about it that way. And I don't have to now. I'm through.

AL: Don't give up, Phil. Not after you've done such good work and come so far in your faith. Keep your eyes on the finish line. Don't drop out of the race now.

PHIL: I've defined my faith by the number of committees I serve on, the number of visits I make in a week, the number of meetings I attend in a month. If I stop, what will count?

AL: Your faith. Your love for the Lord. And I'm not saying you should drop out totally. Just gear down a little. Pick and choose. And look for new roads. Like sharing ice cream with your neighbor.

PHIL: People will think I'm wimping out if I start dropping off committees.

AL: Who are you living your life for, Phil? Those people or the Lord?

PHIL: You're right, Al. Thanks for the guidance. I better get going.

AL: Got a meeting to get to?

PHIL: Nope. I'm going to go have ice cream with my neighbor.

(AL and PHIL shake hands. As Phil exits:)

AL: Just remember to pace yourself. And happy sprinting!

The Deeds to the Property

Characters: Howard, Ms. Mains
Costumes: Contemporary

(A government office. Ms. MAINS sits at a desk with a sign that reads "Registrar of Deeds."
HOWARD enters and approaches her.)

HOWARD: Excuse me?

Ms. MAINS: *(looking up from her work)* Hello. May I help you?

HOWARD: I hope so. I bought a piece of land a couple of weeks ago, and I was told I had to come here and get the deed transferred to my name.

Ms. MAINS: Yes, sir, that is correct procedure. I'll be happy to help you. Won't you have a seat?

(HOWARD sits and Ms. MAINS pulls out some forms.)

Ms. MAINS *(CONT)*: Now. Do you know the legal property description?

HOWARD: You bet. It's the north 40 acres of the south 80 acres of the west half of the northeast fractional quarter of section 4, Clinton Township.

Ms. MAINS: Got it.

HOWARD: Beautiful piece of land. I'm thinking of starting a bed and breakfast.

Ms. MAINS: How nice. Now, if I can just see the deed, we'll be all set.

HOWARD: The deed?

Ms. MAINS: Yes, sir. The deed.

HOWARD: I don't have the deed.

Ms. MAINS: I'm sorry, sir, but I can't transfer the property deed if I don't have the deed.

HOWARD: But I own the property.

Ms. MAINS: But how do I know that you own it?

HOWARD: I can tell you all about it. There's a nice little well in the southeast corner of the lot, the kind you crank the bucket down into. There's a beautiful field of Kentucky bluegrass in the front that makes you want to spend the rest of your life going barefoot. And smack dab in the middle is a white frame house with four bedrooms, a wraparound porch with two porch swings, and a big bay window in the living room . . .

Ms. MAINS: Sir, I appreciate the fact that you can describe the lot and its contents to me with such loving detail, but the fact remains that I must see the actual deed.

HOWARD: I'm telling you more than the deed would.

Ms. MAINS: It's the law, sir.

HOWARD: Bureaucracy raises its narrow little mind again.

Ms. MAINS: These procedures were established for your protection, sir.

HOWARD: This is protecting? I'd hate to have you against me.

Ms. MAINS: Sir, what is stopping someone else who's familiar with the lot from coming in here half an hour from now, describing the lot in similar detail, and laying claim to it?

HOWARD: *(pause, then)* That possibility hadn't occurred to me.

Ms. MAINS: The deed shows me you're not some impostor, pretending to be the owner of the property. It shows me you are truly who you say you are.

HOWARD: Thank you for your concern. I'll be back with the deed.

(HOWARD exits. Ms. MAINS turns to the audience.)

Ms. MAINS: "What good is it . . . if a man claims to have faith but has no deeds? Can such faith save him? Suppose a brother or sister is without clothes and daily food. If one of you says to him, 'Go, I wish you well; keep warm and well fed,' but does nothing about his physical needs, what good is it? In the same way, faith by itself, if it is not accompanied by action, is dead."[26]

[26]James 2:14-17

Looking for the Perfect Church

Characters: Sheila, Bob
Costumes: Contemporary

(Bob sits at the kitchen table. There's a phone on the table in front of him. Sheila enters with the Yellow Pages. Sheila sits down with Bob and begins scanning a page in the directory.)

Sheila: I suppose we should start from the top, with the A's. Let's see, Anglican. Apostolic. Assembly. Let's try this one. *(She dials a number and waits a moment.)* Hello? Yes, my husband and I are looking for a church. What time are your Sunday services? . . . eleven o'clock for morning worship? Can you guarantee that the benediction will be given by noon?

(Sheila looks at the phone in surprise and hangs up.)

Bob: What?

Sheila: She laughed.

(Bob takes the phone book from Sheila and scans the page.)

Bob: Some people have a weird sense of humor. Here's one. *(He dials.)* Hello? My wife and I are looking for a church, and we were wondering if you guarantee that your morning worship services will be over by noon? . . . You do! . . . I see, and since you televise your services, you have to keep to a strict schedule. Well, do you also guarantee that your pastor will be relevant, entertaining, and not too threatening in his sermons? . . . Very good. What about the sanctuary? Air-conditioned? . . . Are the pews padded? . . . Theatre style? Wonderful! How about baptism? Is it immersion or sprinkling? . . . Neither? Okay, thank you very much.

(Bob hangs up. Sheila takes the book from him.)

Sheila: They don't baptize?

Bob: Once a year, they have a pool party, but that's the only time they do anything involving water.

Sheila: Next. *(She dials.)* Hi, we're looking for a church, and we were wondering about yours. Are you biblically sound and fundamentally based? . . . What about sin? . . . You don't like it. Good. In that case, can you guarantee that all your youth activities, including parties and hayrides, are sin free? . . . Thank you

(Sheila hangs up. Bob takes the book.)

Bob: Well?

Sheila: He said I should get real. No youth gathering is ever or can ever be completely sin free.

Bob: What kind of kids go to that church?

Sheila: Apparently, ones that sin!

Bob: *(He dials.)* Hi there. The wife and I are looking for a new church, and we wanted to know if yours is large enough that we won't stand out, but still small enough that we can get a lot of attention from the pastor . . . I see. And stewardship. Is your budget large enough to allow creative programming without being so tight that someone's going to be hitting us up for money all the time? . . . Okay. I understand. Thank you.

(Bob hangs up. Sheila takes the book.)

Sheila: *(dialing)* Another bunch that expects you to give regularly, huh?

Bob: I don't know who puts these ideas in people's heads.

Sheila: *(into phone)* Hi. Do you guarantee that your services are over by noon? . . . Are you in a location with easy access to the highway? . . . Modern facilities? . . . Quality programs for all ages? . . . Wonderful. One last question. Do you use the true and faithful translation of the Bible, the King James Version, or one of those modern knockoffs? . . . I see. Thank you.

(SHEILA hangs up.)

BOB: They don't use King James?

SHEILA: They use the New International Version. And I had such hope for them.

BOB: Forget it. I bet they're not even really Christian.

SHEILA: Bob, we're never going to find the perfect church.

BOB: Don't be silly, Sheila. It's out there somewhere.

SHEILA: I'm not sure anymore. I thought our last church was perfect until they took two offerings in one day.

BOB: I had already suspected. I saw the pastor with sermon notes, all typed out on three-by-five cards. Imagine the gall to get into the pulpit with notes, rather than letting the Spirit speak through you freely.

SHEILA: And they wonder why no one goes to church anymore.

BOB: It's because they can't find one! But we can't despair, Sheila. We just have to keep looking. If we expect perfection, we'll find it. And I bet we aren't the only ones. There are probably thousands of people out there looking for the perfect church. If that many people want it, it must exist. So we'll keep looking. Are we in agreement?

SHEILA: Perfect agreement.